Table of Contents

FROM PRETTY TO PUNKED
Fashion Through The Decades 4

ALL DOLLED UP
The 1920s and 1930s 6

COOL CAT
The 1940s and 1950s 56

FAR OUT
The 1960s and 1970s 106

PREPPED AND PUNKED
The 1980s and 1990s 156

RETRO FASHIONS ARE
MODERN FASHIONS 206

INDEX 208

1

FROM PRETTY TO PUNKED *Fashion* THROUGH THE DECADES

Take a look inside your closet. The clothes there reflect your personality, taste, and style. They also reflect the trends of today. But look closer. You likely have separate pieces that you pair together, such as sweaters and skirts. Look at the cuffed jeans and capris folded in your drawer. Have any leopard prints hiding in your wardrobe? Or maybe some leggings or large, dangling earrings?

Believe it or not, the trends people are wearing now aren't entirely new. Shorter skirts and sleeveless fashions stole the scene in the 1920s. Leather jackets and jeans were a rebellious trend in the 1950s. Big hairstyles and bold, colorful makeup grew from the '80s punk movement. The styles of these decades left a lasting impression on fashion. You can't deny that the looks are timeless. And that's why we still love to wear them.

You can bring even more of these iconic styles into your look. From the way you do your hair to the clothes you wear, what was old is new again!

Fashion FORWARD

Creating Your Look With the Best of Vintage Style

by Rebecca Langston-George,
Allison Crotzer Kimmel,
Lori Luster,
and Liz Sonneborn

CAPSTONE PRESS
a capstone imprint

Published by Capstone Young Readers,
1710 Roe Crest Drive, North Mankato, Minnesota 56003
www.capstoneyoungreaders.com

Library of Congress Cataloging-in-Publication Data
Cataloging-in-publication information is on file with the Library of Congress.
ISBN: 978-1-62370-062-1 (paperback)

Editorial Credits
Jennifer Besel and Abby Colich, editors; Tracy Davies McCabe, designer;
Marcie Spence, media researcher; Jennifer Walker, production specialist

Printed in China by Nordica.
1013/CA21301920
092013 007745NORDS14

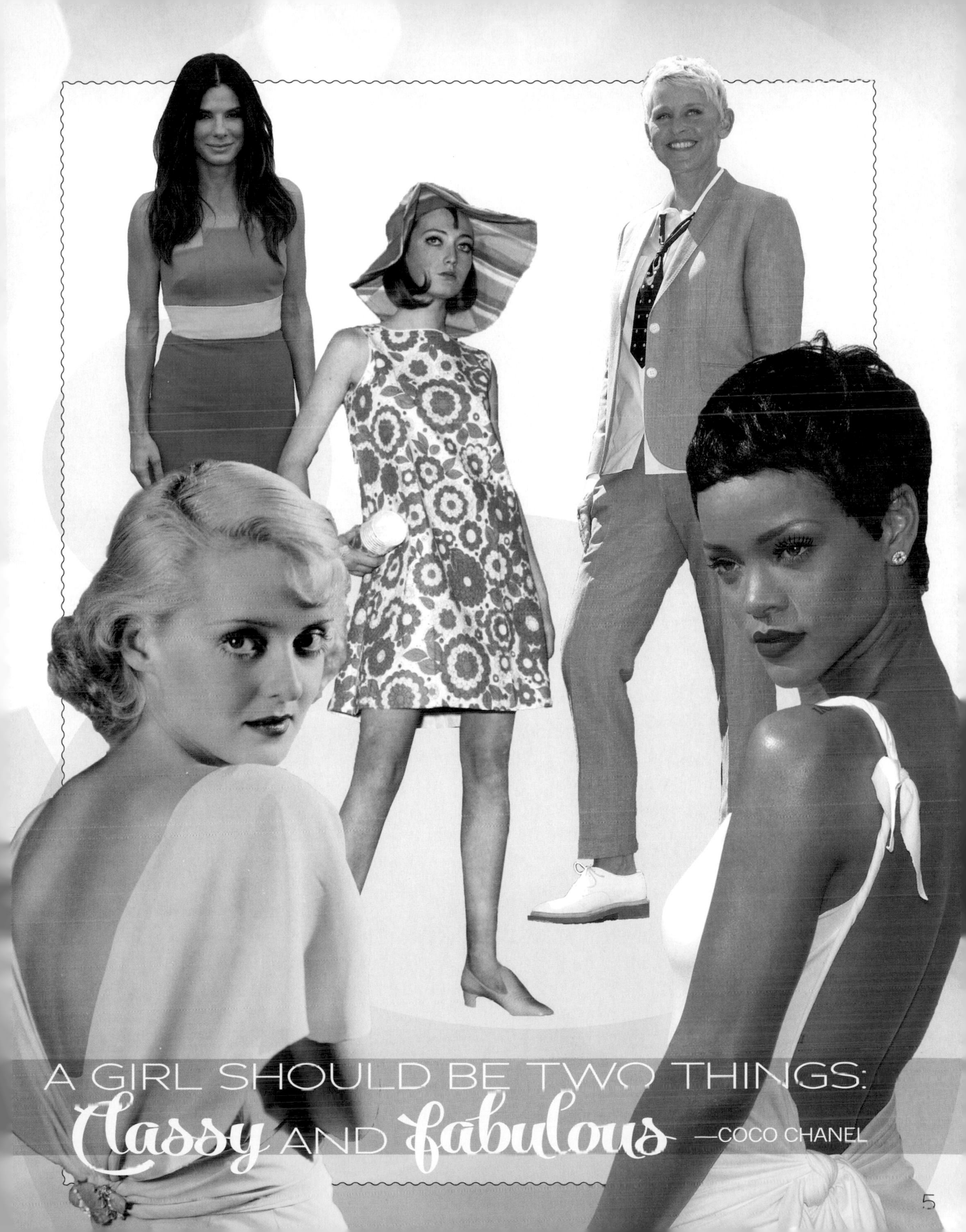
A GIRL SHOULD BE TWO THINGS:
Classy AND fabulous —COCO CHANEL

2

All Dolled Up

The 1920s and 1930s

The Roaring Twenties were a time of wild excess. The music was loud, and the dances were shocking. Young women wore shorter dresses and hairstyles than ever before. Some people called the fashions scandalous.

Wild dances such as the Charleston swept across the United States. These new dances required clothes that allowed dancers' arms and legs to move freely. If you had to sum up 1920s style in one word, it would be legs. Hems rose as high as the knees for the first time in modern history. Short dresses even replaced long dresses for fancy evening wear. Legs that had long been covered by full skirts were now everywhere.

Major law changes during this decade gave people both freedom and restriction. In August 1920 Congress passed the 19th Amendment, granting women the right to vote. This new freedom was a sign of the changing times. Women wouldn't be held back any longer. The loose, relaxed styles were just one outward sign of this new attitude.

In January 1920, the 18th Amendment banned alcohol. Prohibition had a deep effect on life in the 1920s. Men and women went to secret speakeasies to party. The popularity of this underground scene led to the rebellious, free-spirited attitude the 1920s is remembered for.

Fabulous Flappers

The daring flapper has been revived today.

No group was more rebellious or free-spirited than the young women called flappers. Flappers were liberal women who drove cars and danced the nights away. They came to symbolize the attitudes of the 1920s.

Flappers wore dresses decorated with rows of fringe or glass beads that swayed in rhythm to their dance moves. No tight waists or corsets for these girls! Instead, they wore boxy shaped dresses with loose, dropped waists. Bare arms swung to the beat of the music.

The daring flapper has been revived today. Katy Perry and Carrie Underwood have both been spotted in flapper inspired clothing.

In June 2012 Perry wore a flapper headband and long pearls. Her peach floor-length evening gown added to the vintage look.

Flapper styles are popular on dance floors too. Celebs on *Dancing with the Stars* often wear beaded outfits that sway with their fancy footwork.

Movies have brought back the carefree and fresh styles of the '20s too. The 2013 movie *The Great Gatsby* showcased fringed flappers. The successful movie had people roaring for the looks themselves. Brands such as Fogal and Brooks Brothers released new lines inspired by the movie. And countless blogs and news shows told viewers how to get the looks for less.

Get the Look

Long strands of beads that swung around while dancing where very popular in the 1920s. A single extra-long strand of beads might be hard to find now. But you can make your own from two shorter strands.

SUPPLIES

- 2 matching strands of beads

1. Lay the two strands end to end on your workspace, overlapping slightly.
2. Where the strands overlap, pull the bottom strand up over the top one to make a circle.
3. Bring the bottom of the strand nearest you up to the circle. Pull it under the circle you just made.
4. Pull until the strand goes all the way through to knot the strands together.

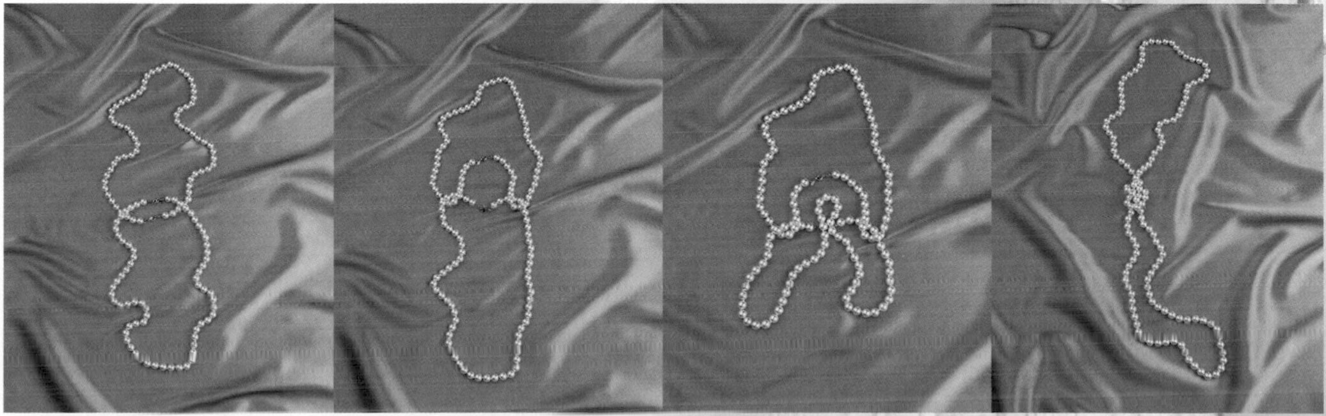

Get the Look

Change a plain summer dress into a flapper sensation. Check your closet or hit the thrift store for a knee-length tank dress. Then add some fringe for a flapper makeover.

SUPPLIES

- sewing measuring tape
- solid-colored knee-length tank dress
- scissors
- 2-inch (5-centimeter) long chainette fringe in a complimentary color to your dress
- pins
- thread to match the fringe
- needle

1. Measure around the bottom of the dress.
2. Add 1 inch (2.5 cm) to your measurement.
3. Cut three pieces of fringe the length you calculated in step 2.
4. Pin one piece of fringe around the bottom of the dress. The ends should overlap in the back, and the fringe should hang below the hem line.
5. Sew the fringe in place, starting in the back and working your way around the dress. When you get back to the end, fold the last ½ inch (1-cm) of fringe under itself and stitch it in place.
6. Pin another row of fringe above the first so they overlap slightly. Sew that row in place.
7. Repeat step 6 to make a third row of fringe. Now you're ready for the dance floor!

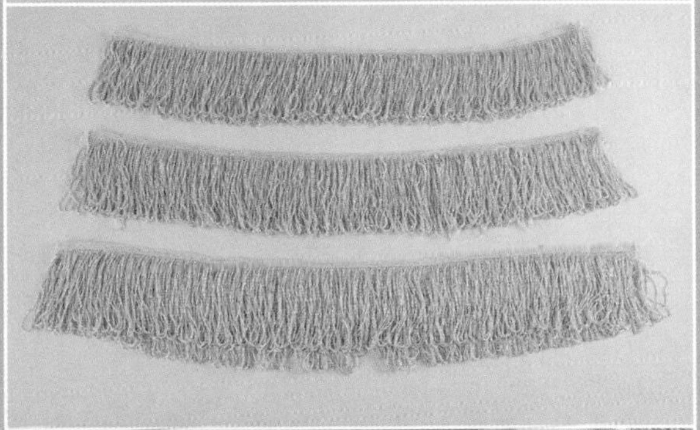

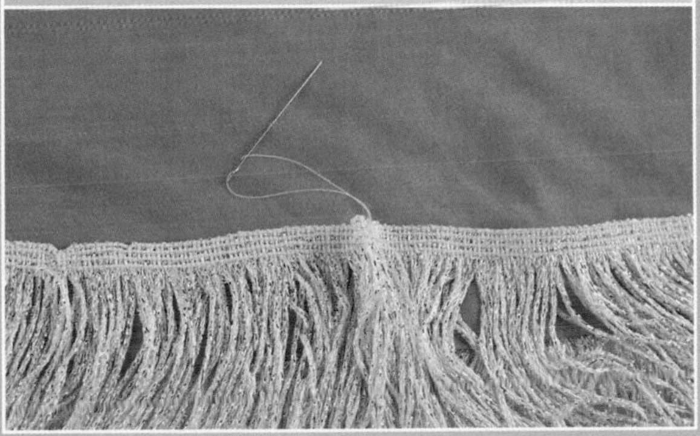

1920s
Hair and Makeup

Just like today's young women, flappers imitated the hairstyles and makeup of popular actresses. Celebs in those days were silent movie stars. Actress Louise Brooks' short bobbed hair was all the rage. Women raced to beauty salons to shake out their hairpins and cut their long hair.

If you think the bobbed hair of the 1920s is out, think again. Take a look at the bob Katie Holmes wore. The inspiration is unmistakable.

Get the Look

Headbands and combs with colorful feathers were popular 1920s accessories. No matter what length you wear your hair, you can jazz up your locks flapper style.

SUPPLIES

- hot glue gun and glue
- two small, colorful feathers
- fancy button with a shank
- ½-inch (1-cm) wide or wider elastic headband
- marker
- needle and thread

1. Hot glue the feathers to the back of the button.
2. Put the headband on. It should go over your hair and across your forehead.
3. While looking in a mirror, make a small dot on the headband where you want the feathers and button to go. They should be off to one side, between your eye and ear.
4. Take off the headband. Sew the button to the headband on the dot you made in step 3.
5. Wear the headband across your forehead flapper style.

Movie stars also introduced women to makeup, which most young women of the time had never worn. Silent actress Clara Bow was famous for her lipstick pout, much like Angelina Jolie is known for her full lips today. Bow's look made young women line up to buy lipstick for the first time. Their parents were horrified!

Get the Look

Silent movie stars made a powerful statement without talking. But their bold pouty lips sure spoke to the audience. To get Clara's perfect pout, all you need is a tube of bright red lipstick. There was no lip liner, gloss, or stain back then. Stand in front of the mirror and pucker up. Apply the lipstick heavily to the middle of your lips. Narrow the line of lipstick as you reach the corners of the lips.

Today's celebs continue the pouty tradition. You're sure to see it on the red carpet and in magazines. Scarlett Johansson, Drew Barrymore, and Taylor Swift have all pulled off the pout.

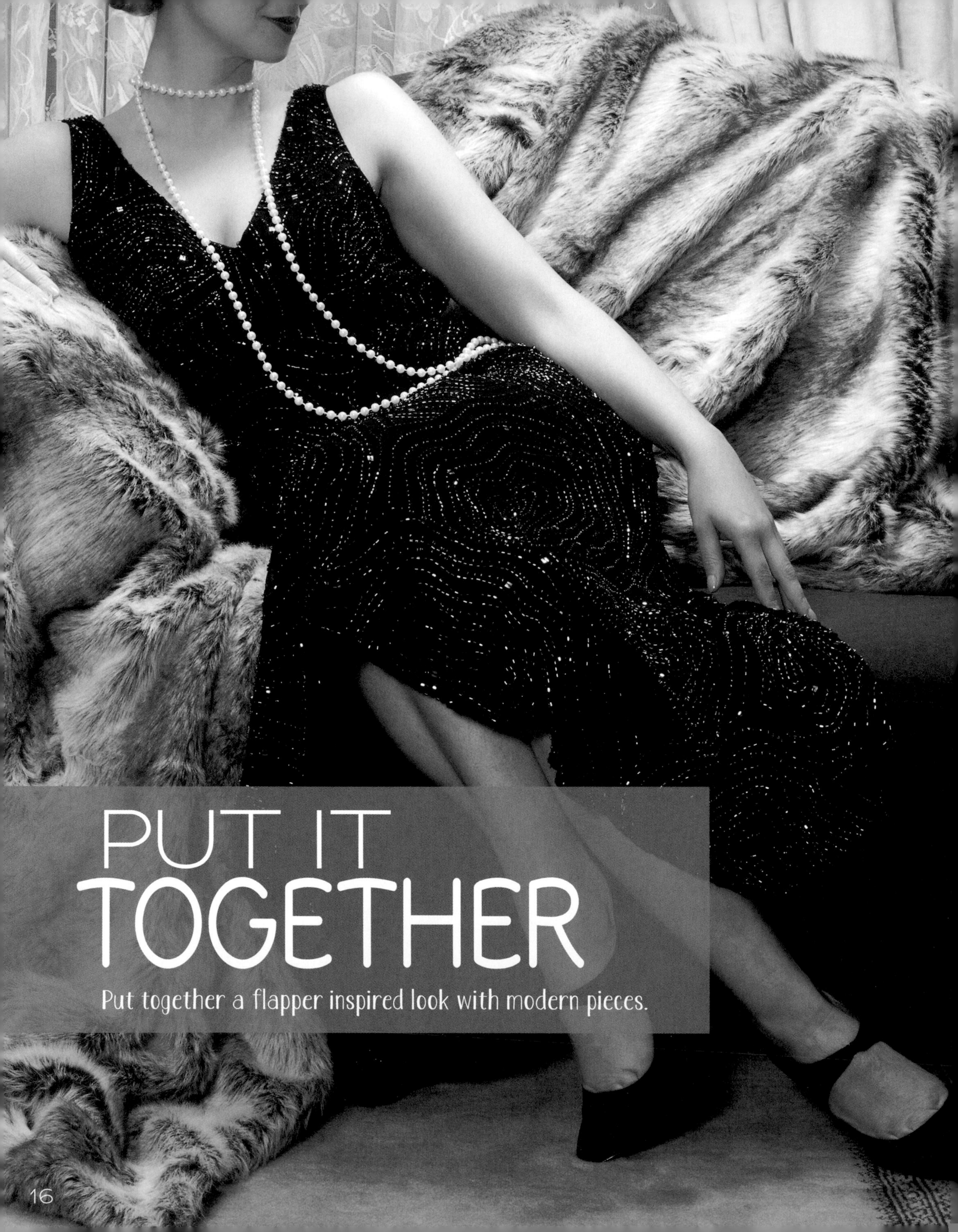

PUT IT TOGETHER

Put together a flapper inspired look with modern pieces.

Party and costume stores often carry 1920s headbands. But you can easily make your own too.

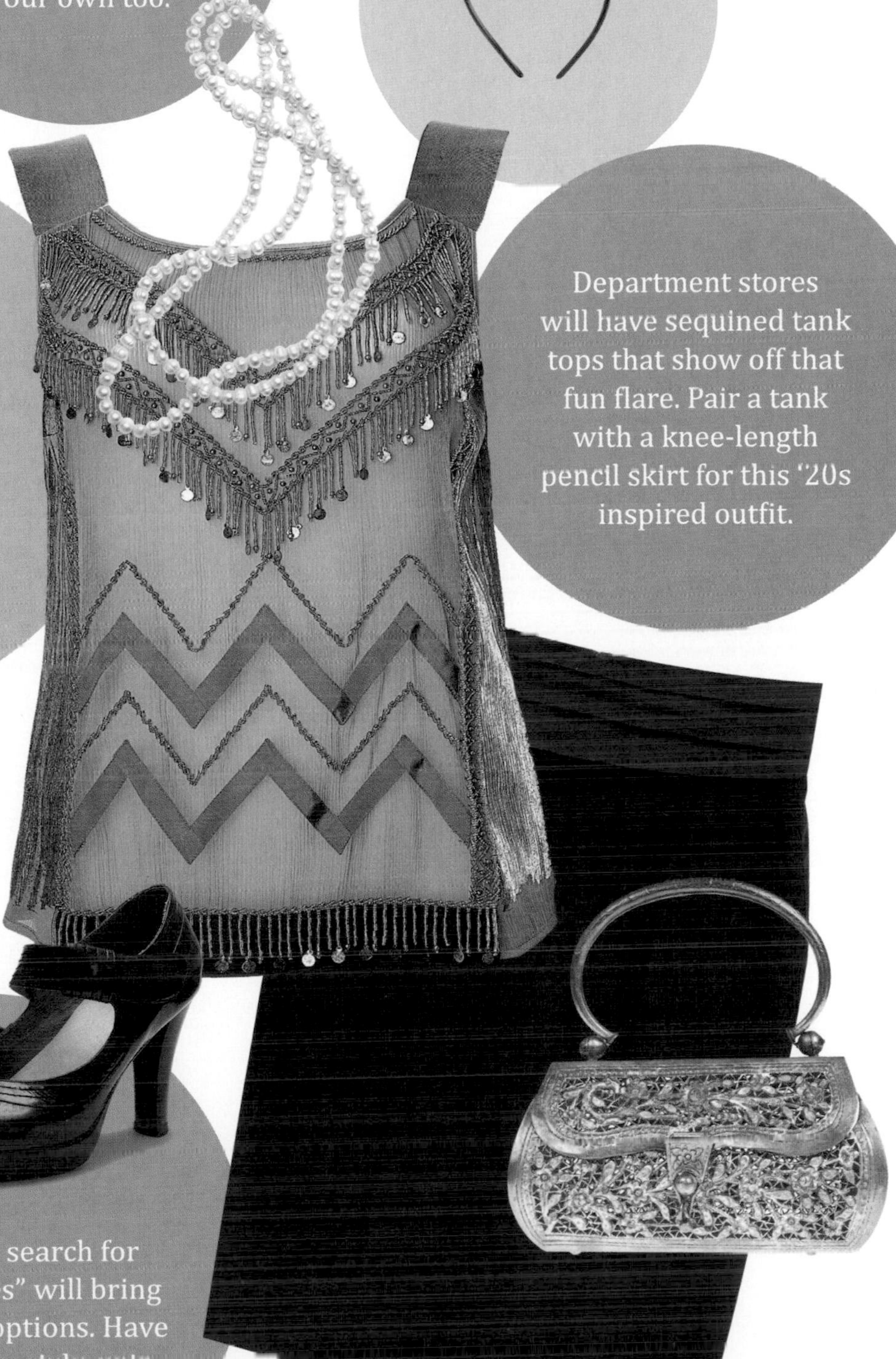

Check accessory shops for long necklaces and flashy beaded bags. Don't forget to check the attic too. You never know what your great-grandma might have saved for you.

Department stores will have sequined tank tops that show off that fun flare. Pair a tank with a knee-length pencil skirt for this '20s inspired outfit.

A quick online search for "Mary Jane shoes" will bring up hundreds of options. Have fun choosing the right pair for you!

Everyday Elegance

The beads and fringe of flapper dresses were perfect for the dance floor. But they weren't very practical for daily life. Women needed comfortable, stylish clothing for everyday wear. One designer who understood this need was Coco Chanel.

Around the beginning of World War I (1914–1918), Chanel began designing clothes using a light knit fabric called jersey. Until then jersey had only been used to make men's underwear. But Chanel liked the soft, stretchy fabric and thought women would find it comfortable. She created women's separates. Chanel's separates, unlike dresses, were outfits made up of individual pieces. Skirts, blouses, and sweaters that can be mixed and matched are called sportswear separates. Much like the loose, flowing flapper dresses, these pieces were unfitted and sporty. The popularity of this fashion proved that the 1920s woman wanted to be both fashionable and able to move.

Today's women still want to be fashionable and comfortable. Everybody, even A-list celebs, still wear sportswear fashions. Nicole Richie's Winter Kate collection even includes throwback fashions inspired by the 1920s' sportswear trend.

COCO CHANEL

Scent-sational

NICOLE RICHIE

Chanel was also one of the first designers to sell her own perfume. She began selling it in her boutique in 1921. It's still available at perfume counters today. You can stir up your own designer fragrance. Go ahead and name it after yourself.

SUPPLIES

- 1 rose
- warm tap water
- large bowl
- slotted spoon
- funnel
- coffee filter
- antique perfume bottle or small, empty plastic bottle
- essential oil, your choice of scent (optional)

1. Pull the rose petals off the stem, and rinse them in cool water.
2. Pour 1 cup (240 milliliters) of very warm tap water into a bowl.
3. Push the petals into the water. Let them sit overnight.
4. In the morning remove the petals from the water with a slotted spoon.
5. If you wish, add up to 10 drops of essential oil to the rose water. Stir gently.
6. Line a funnel with a coffee filter. Strain the rose water into the perfume bottle. Use the perfume within a few days.

The Gatsby Look

Designer Jean Patou took Chanel's sporty separates to another level—actual sports! In 1921 he created a tennis outfit for French player Suzanne Lenglen. She wore a knee-length pleated white skirt and sleeveless white cardigan. It made a huge sensation. Lenglen could move like today's tennis stars in her new clothing. And she looked fabulous doing it.

Everyday fashions began to copy Lenglen's look. Today this sporty style is called the Great Gatsby look. The term comes from F. Scott Fitzgerald's 1925 novel *The Great Gatsby*. Stars such as Blake Lively keep the pleated skirt fashionable. Separates that can be mixed and matched are the staples of today's wardrobe. The separates in your closet have a lot in common with the sporty trend of the 1920s.

PUT IT TOGETHER

Pair these modern pieces together, and show off your own Gatsby look.

Grab a plain white T-shirt from your closet.

Look for a sporty pleated skirt in a local store's sportswear department.

Find a long solid-color cardigan from a neighborhood thrift shop.

Tie on some cute white canvas tennis shoes. Sometimes you can even find these at a dollar store.

Dig through your grandma's closet to find a vintage cloche hat. Accessory stores carry these too.

Grab a long, knit white or striped scarf to finish off the look.

Athletic Clothing

The popularity of Lenglen's tennis outfit inspired new trends. Patou and other designers made clothes for other sports. Finally female athletes had clothing that they could play in. No more long, full skirts and big hats. Women could buy golf outfits, ski outfits, and stylish bathing suits in addition to tennis wear. The public's opinion of the outdoors changed with the styles.

In earlier times women stayed out of the sun. They wore large brimmed hats and gloves to cover up. Suddenly sunshine and outdoor sports became stylish.

Of course, athletic clothing is a booming business even today. Tennis star Venus Williams' clothing line EleVen features trendy clothes for active women. Yesterday's sports clothes definitely paved the way for today's gym clothes and yoga pants.

Wearing Pants

Women almost never wore pants before the late 1920s. But the carefree '20s changed that too. Women's pants started as casual wear for the wealthy. Swimsuit coverings called bathing pajamas became popular. They were followed by lounging pajamas. These pajamas weren't meant for sleep. However, women didn't wear them in public. Lounging pajamas were flowing, comfortable items to wear around the house. Wearing pants outside the house would start to take off in the 1930s.

LOUNGING PAJAMAS

The Little Black Dress

Chanel also popularized the black dress fashion trend that remains a must-have to this day. The "Little Black Dress,"or LBD, became a hit in the 1920s. Chanel's LBDs were fashionable, yet simple. The dresses could go from afternoon to evening wear with the simple switch of a hat. Women loved them!

Chanel's first LBD design had long sleeves and was made of wool, velvet, or satin. But the dress soon came in many variations, including short sleeves and sleeveless and could be made with chiffon or lace.

The LBD trend is a long-lasting one. In fact, fashion gurus today still say that no wardrobe is complete without one. And like all trends, celebrities are on the front lines.

MOLLY RINGWALD 1987

PRINCESS DIANA 1995

HALLE BERRY 2012

AUDREY HEPBURN
1961

ACCESSORIZING

Just like today, the modern 1920s woman enjoyed accessorizing with scarves, hats, and costume jewelry. A scarf was essential for the Gatsby look. The perfect scarf for the sporty look was long and narrow. It was typically knitted and often fringed at the bottom. Plain white scarves or horizontally striped ones were popular.

But how a woman wore it was just as important as which scarf she chose. The scarf was wrapped around the neck once. One end was worn down the front and the other down the back.

In the 2010s scarves came roaring back as a fashion craze. Today's scarves come in all kinds of styles and are tied in hundreds of ways. But it's fun to see the 1920s scarf trend revived in a new way.

KELLY ROWLAND
SINGER

Get the Look

Make your own Gatsby scarf. No-sew blanket fleece from the fabric store is perfect for this project.

SUPPLIES

- white fleece, 7 inches (18 cm) wide by 58 inches (147 cm) long
- ruler
- pencil
- scissors
- tape

1. Lay the fleece across your workspace so one short end faces you.
2. Measure 2½ inches (6 cm) up from the end, and make a light pencil mark on the fleece.
3. Lay a piece of tape across the width of the fabric at the mark you made in step 2.
4. Measure ¼ inch (.6 cm) from the left side below the tape line. Make a light pencil mark. Continue measuring across the width of the fleece, making marks at ¼-inch (.6-cm) intervals.
5. Create fringe by cutting the fleece from the bottom edge up to the tape, following the marks made in step 4. Remove the tape.
6. Repeat steps 2 through 5 on the other end of the fleece.

Costume jewelry was another popular accessory of the 1920s. Always the trend setter, Chanel sold costume jewelry as well as clothing. Inexpensive jewelry was not entirely new. It had been around since the 1800s. But it served a different purpose. Costume jewelry before the '20s was made to imitate real gems that a woman already owned. A woman might wear the cheaper copy while keeping her "real" jewelry locked in the safe.

Chanel made costume jewelry fashionable for everyone. Glass pearls and imitation gold were her signature pieces. In her words, "A girl should be two things: classy and fabulous." If you like looking fabulous, but don't want to break the bank, you can thank Chanel for affordable jewelry.

Hats really topped off the sporty outfits of the day. The hat style that ruled the 1920s was the cloche. A cloche fit snugly over the forehead. Covering the back of the neck and the ears, it was decorated with ribbons, beads, or feathers. Its popularity might be due to how well it fit over a bobbed haircut. Bobbed hair and cloche hats were made for each other.

Like scarves, cloche hats aren't hard to find these days. Model Marisa Miller wore one to the 2011 Kentucky Derby. Kelly Osbourne and Sarah Jessica Parker have been caught wearing these stunning 1920s hats too.

A GIRL SHOULD BE TWO THINGS: CLASSY AND FABULOUS

CRISTA B. ALLEN
ACTRESS

LEIGHTON MEESTER
ACTRESS

Get the Look

Add some decoration to a modern cloche hat to get that 1920s flair.

SUPPLIES

- leaf-shaped cookie cutter
- 3 sheets of felt, in complimentary colors to your hat
- pencil or marker
- scissors
- needle and thread
- colorful flat button
- hot glue gun and glue
- cloche hat, often found in the fall or winter at accessory stores

1. Lay the cookie cutter on a piece of felt. Trace around the cutter. Trace three leaves on each sheet of felt.
2. Cut out the felt leaves.
3. Arrange the leaves in a flower shaped pile, so you can see each one. Place the button in the center.
4. Sew the flower together through the button holes.
5. Hot glue the flower to one side of the hat.

Fancy Footwork

Today's shoes also share similarities with the shoes your great-grandmothers wore. Look for shoes with rounded edges, closed toes, and medium-high chunky heels. Mary Jane shoes with a strap across the front will give you a vintage look. So will T-straps, which have a vertical strap in addition to the Mary Jane strap.

Another modern shoe style that gets its look from the '20s is the shootie. Shootie is a combination of the word shoe and boot. Modern shooties come up the foot all the way to the ankle. Vintage ones aren't quite as tall. But they all give a fantastic flapper feel.

SLIMMER CLOTHES FOR SLIMMER TIMES

The good times of the Roaring Twenties came to a sudden halt in October 1929. The stock market crashed, and the world plummeted into the Great Depression (1929–1939). Many people lost their jobs and their homes. No one felt like dancing anymore. And no one had extra cash for fancy clothes. The feathers, fringe, and beads of the carefree flapper days went out of style.

As the nation's mood fell so did dress hems. Knee-length dresses and skirts were replaced by hems that fell to mid-calf. The importance of legs in the last decade changed to an interest in feminine curves. Boxy, dropped waist dresses were out. They were replaced by more fitted clothing that hugged the waist.

Belted dresses showed off a slim waist. Separates also became more closely fitted to the body. The long, loose cardigans of the '20s turned into shorter, shapelier sweaters and jackets.

These trends didn't die out when the economy improved. Belted dresses and short jackets are still everywhere. Michelle Obama rocks the belted, longer hem look. Nicki Minaj and Catherine, Duchess of Cambridge, have worn '30s inspired jackets.

CATHERINE
DUCHESS OF CAMBRIDGE

PUT IT TOGETHER

During the Great Depression, people got the latest news by purchasing newspapers from boys on the street. The 1930s newsboy look is easy to re-create.

Modern newsboy caps are popular. You can find them at just about any accessory or department store.

Raid your brother's or dad's closets for a plain white T-shirt.

Find some colorful suspenders to complement your socks. Grandpa's closet or a thrift store would be great places to look for these.

A pair of khakis that you already have will work fine. Just roll them up to mid-calf.

A funky pair of knee-high socks are the key to this look.

Popular Pants

Practical and comfortable, pants became common casual wear by the mid-1930s. The most popular style was the sailor pant. These wide-legged, high-waisted pants didn't have zippers. Instead they were fastened with two rows of buttons at the front. The 1930s woman completed the look with sweaters.

Even this retro fashion is still very much in style. Christina Aguilera and Gwen Stefani made waves sporting sailor pants. The Ralph Lauren brand sells several wide-leg, high-waisted pants too.

CHRISTINA AGUILERA

Bare No More

The bare arms of the flapper days left with the 1920s. The conservative sleeves of the '30s came in many styles. Many of the same sleeve types hanging in your closet today were popular then. Long sleeves came plain, cuffed, or banded at the wrist. Short sleeves might have bows, cuffs, or lace in a contrasting color. The loose, fluttering sleeve that falls just below the shoulder was popular too.

Get the Look

Give an old T-shirt new life with a retro 1930s look.

SUPPLIES

- long sleeve solid color T-shirt
- ruler
- piece of chalk
- scissors
- needle
- thread
- pins

1. Turn the shirt inside out. Lay it flat, and smooth out any wrinkles. Make sure the seams are lined up.
2. Lay the ruler at the top of one sleeve where it meets the shoulder. Measure down the sleeve. Make a chalk mark at 5 inches (13 cm) and 10 inches (25 cm).

3. Chalk a line from the armpit seam to the 10-inch (25-cm) mark. Cut along this line to remove the sleeve. Set the cut off sleeve aside.
4. Chalk a line from the top end of the now shortened sleeve up to the 5-inch (13-cm) mark. Cut a slit up to the 5-inch mark.
5. Tie the two sides of the slit together in a double knot. Voila! You now have a short bow-tie sleeve.
6. Repeat steps 1–5 on the other sleeve. Then turn the shirt right-side out.
7. Grab one of the cut off sleeves. Lay it flat and smooth out any wrinkles. Cut off the hem and the side seam.
8. Cut two long strips from the sleeve. They should be as long as the sleeve and 2 inches (5 cm) wide.
9. Place one strip on top of the other. Sew a seam along one of the 2-inch (5-cm) ends.
10. Open the strips up into one long strip. Press the seam open with an iron.
11. Lay the strip horizontally on your work space. Starting with the long top edge, roll the strip into a burrito. Pin the middle of the fabric roll to the middle of the T-shirt's neck.
12. Sew the fabric roll to the T-shirt with a few stitches.
13. Tie the fabric roll into a bow.

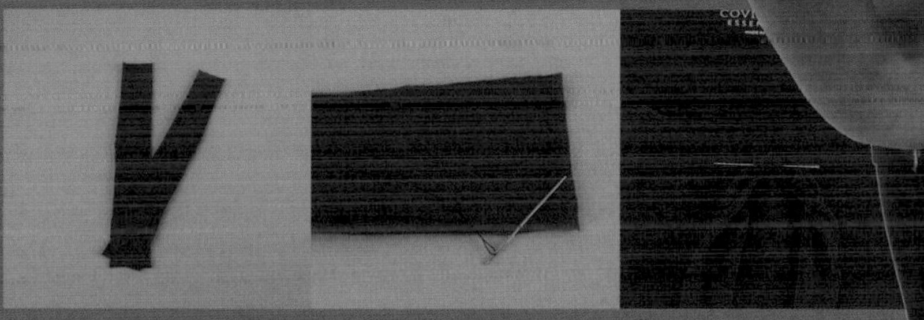

Making Waves

Hems and sleeves weren't the only fashions that dropped during the Great Depression. In the 1930s women let their bobbed hair grow longer. Soft, wavy hairdos replaced straight, slick bobs. A style called finger waves became the hair sensation of the decade. Finger waves were S-shaped curves that zigzagged down the side of the face. Some women got their hair set in permanent waves at the beauty parlor. But to save money, many women set their hair in finger waves at home.

Beautiful hair never goes out of style. Finger waves are a classic. You'll often see modern versions of these waves on the red carpet. Taylor Swift regularly wears finger waves in her hair. She's even picked up a few Grammy awards sporting the look. Model Tyra Banks also likes to experiment with this look.

Get the Look

Finger waves are a tricky look to create at first. But after some practice, you'll have the sleek, retro look that will make heads turn.

SUPPLIES

- a fine-toothed comb
- hair gel
- several long duckbill or alligator hair clips
- curlers

1. Start with clean, damp (but not wet) hair. Use a comb to make a clean side part.
2. Comb a generous amount of gel through the hair on the left side of the part.
3. Press your right pointer finger firmly along the part. The finger should point toward your forehead.
4. Lay your middle finger on your hair. Pinch up the hair between your pointer and middle fingers to create a little wave. Press your fingers down firmly on your head to hold the hair in place.
5. As you hold down the hair, use your other hand to gently comb the hair below the pinched wave toward the back of your head.
6. Put the comb down and place clips where your fingers were holding down the hair. The clips should point toward your forehead.
7. Press your pointer finger firmly on your head just below the lowest clip. Repeat steps 4–6 to create another wave. This time comb the hair below the wave toward your face, and point the clips toward the back of your head.
8. Continue making waves down the side of your head, alternating the direction of the combing and clips.
9. Repeat steps 2–8 on the other side of your head.
10. Comb gel through the hair left in the back. Roll it in curlers.
11. Let your hair dry completely with the clips and curlers in place. Then remove the clips and curlers. Use your fingers to brush through the back of your hair.

GOLDEN AGE OF STYLE

Real life during the Great Depression was difficult. But life on the big screen was adventurous. A movie ticket cost just a quarter in the mid-1930s. It was a cheap way to forget your troubles for a couple of hours. The public packed theaters to watch their favorite stars. Movie tickets today cost more than a quarter, but they're still popular entertainment. And movie stars still rule the world of glamorous fashion.

Red carpet fashions date back to the first Academy Awards. It was held at the Hollywood Roosevelt Hotel in 1929. Stars wore long, elegant evening gowns. Floor-length gowns that hugged the body were the style. Legs were covered but backs were daringly bare. Watch any red carpet event, and you can see this is a trend that continues today.

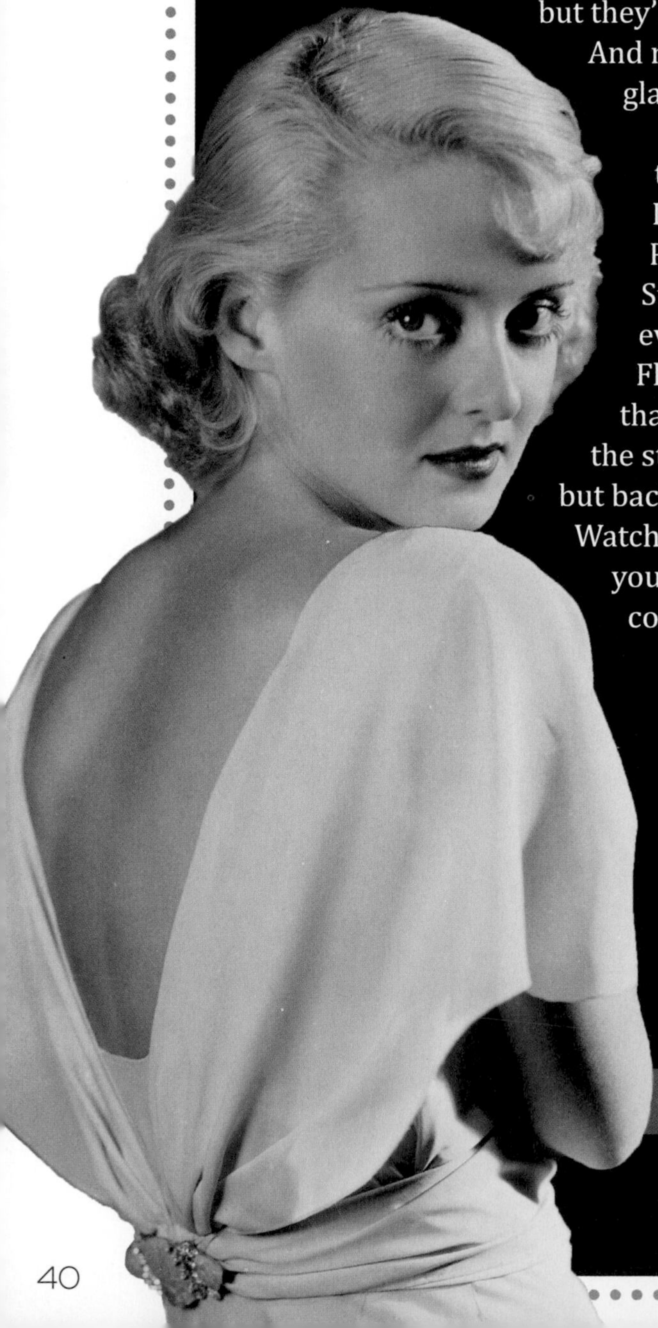

BETTE DAVIS

RIHANNA

Get the Look

You don't have to wait for a red carpet invitation to try the bare back look. Keep it young and modern by updating the back of a T-shirt.

SUPPLIES

- a piece of paper
- scissors
- a T-shirt in your choice of color and style
- pins
- chalk
- seam sealant for fabric
- hot glue gun and glue
- gemstones

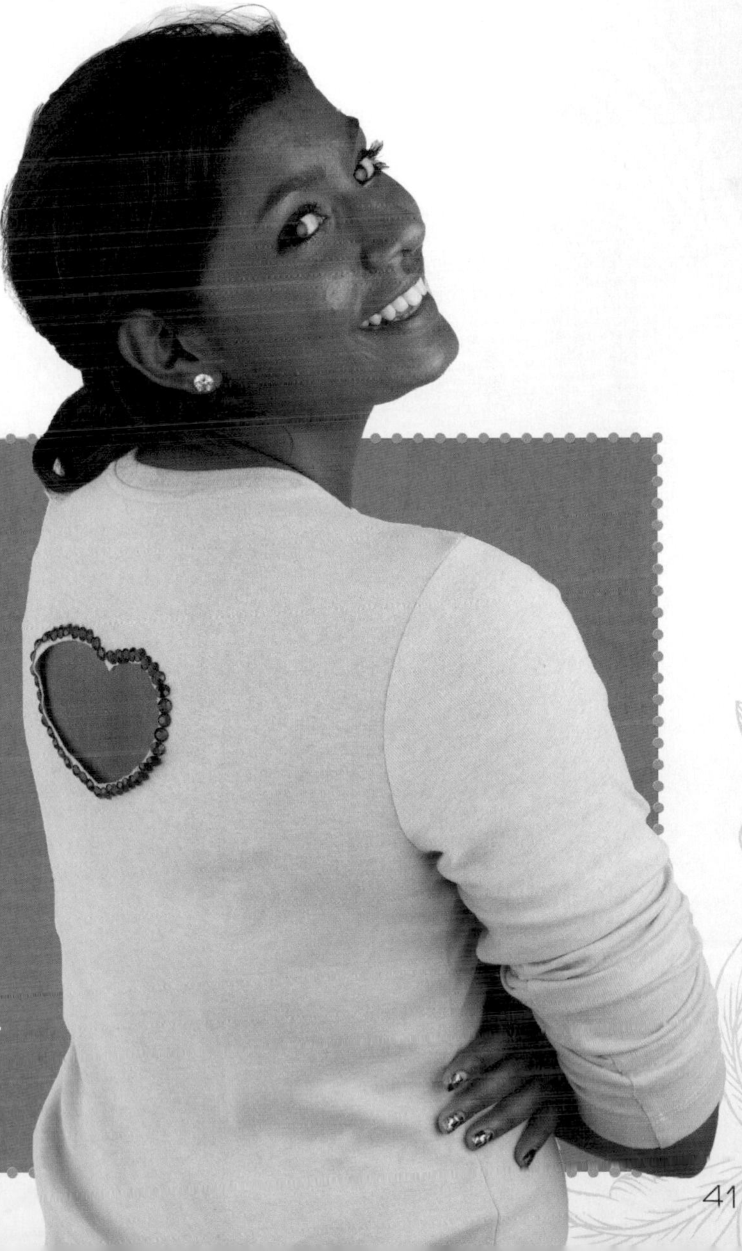

1. Fold the piece of paper in half. Cut out half of a fat heart shape. Unfold the heart.
2. Turn the shirt inside out. Pin the heart on the upper back side of the shirt.
3. Trace a chalk line around the heart. Remove the paper pattern.
4. Cut along the line to make a heart that gives a peek at your back.
5. Turn the shirt right side out. Use seam sealant around the cut edges of the heart using package directions.
6. Hot glue gemstones around the heart to give it a finished look.

A Little Bias

Hollywood's 1930s glam styles were a stark contrast to the dim real world. Parisian designer Madeleine Vionnet played a huge role in those stunning styles. She created dresses by cutting fabric at an angle across its weave. This method, called the bias cut, allowed fabric to drape and follow a body's curves.

While bias cutting might not sound very exciting, the effect it had on fashion and society was shocking. Dresses in the 1930s began to cling tightly to bare skin. Every natural curve of the body was displayed. Garments no longer hid the female form—they celebrated it.

The glamorous starlet look is still around today. Look for long, simple shapes that hug the body. The focus is on the cut and drape of the dress. These gowns are often a solid color. Bare backs are another clue to a vintage look.

Some of the stars who have been spotted looking like they walked off the 1930s red carpet include Charlize Theron, Kate Winslet, and Jessica Chastain. Angelina Jolie's gown for the 2012 Golden Globes is an example of a modern starlet look. It was a draped blush-colored gown with a red triangle at the neckline.

The glamorous starlet look is still around today.

PENNY SINGLETON

Get the Look

Women of the '30s wore makeup more frequently than their 1920s sisters. In addition to lipstick, mascara and eye shadow were added. Pink tones were all the rage.

To get the look, dab pink cream blush on your cheeks along the cheekbones. Add a shimmery pink eye shadow over the top of the eyelid. Apply mascara to the top eyelashes only. Finish with loose powder from a powder puff. Finally, give your lips a thin coat of raspberry colored lipstick.

IT **SUITS** YOU

MARLENE DIETRICH

ELLEN DEGENERES

It was a new kind of rebellion.

Another Hollywood look to emerge during this time was the masculine look. With the popularity of pants, some stars took to dressing in men's wear. Marlene Dietrich wore this look on and off screen. It became her signature look. This controversial style blurred the lines between men's and women's clothing. It was a new kind of rebellion.

The masculine look for female stars is still popular today. Kirsten Dunst, Penelope Cruz, and Rihanna are just a few celebs who have rocked the suit look. Mary-Kate and Ashley Olsen's fashion line Elizabeth and James makes trendy suits for the female body. But Ellen DeGeneres and Diane Keaton are probably the most famous names pulling off this look today.

PUT IT TOGETHER

Looking like a movie star doesn't mean you have to strut around in a floor-length evening gown. You can wear Marlene Dietrich's famous masculine look anywhere.

Top off your look with a funky fedora from the accessory store.

Borrow a white button-down collared shirt from your mom.

Raid your dad's closet for a fun tie to add a splash of color.

Find a pair of dress pants and a matching blazer at the thrift store.

REALLY UNREAL FASHIONS

Everyone from tennis stars to actresses influenced fashion design in the 1920s and 1930s. So it's no surprise that artists were interested in fashion too.

In the mid-1930s painters such as Salvador Dali were creating art in a new style called surrealism. Surreal art was often inspired by dreams. The pictures contained unusual things. Sometimes shocking or funny, the art was always unique. Dali called his art "hand-painted dream photographs."

Dali brought this style to fashion runways by working with clothing designer Elsa Schiaparelli. Together they made humorous clothing, jewelry, and accessories. One of Dali's most famous jewelry pieces for Schiaparelli was a brooch. The brooch looked like a pair of red rhinestone covered lips around a row of pearl teeth.

Get the Look

Make your own copy of Dali's famous lips brooch.

SUPPLIES

- pencil
- white poster board
- scissors
- adhesive red gemstone strips
- adhesive pearl strip
- hot glue gun and glue
- flat back pin

1. Draw the shape of a pair of lips onto the poster board. The drawing should be about 3 inches (8 cm) wide and 2.5 inches (6 cm) tall. Cut the lips out.
2. Press the red gemstone strips along the bottom edge of the poster board shape. Be careful to follow the shape of the lips.
3. Continue covering the lips with gemstones, working from the outside edge into the center. Leave the center empty.
4. Press on a line of pearls in the center to make teeth.
5. Turn the project over, and hot glue the pin to the back.

TOGETHER, SCHIAPARELLI AND DALI CREATED SOME MEMORABLE CLOTHES.

The humorous surreal style was often an illusion. Schiaparelli popularized the style called trompe l'oeil, which creates a 3D effect in clothing. Schiaparelli herself first turned heads by wearing a tromp l'oeil sweater. It looked like it had a real bow tied at the neck. But it was an illusion. The art was knitted into the sweater's design.

Trompe l'oeil fashions are still trendy. Paris Hilton, among other celebs, has pulled off this fashion magic. Designer Mary Katrantzou uses the style to make clothes that need no jewelry.

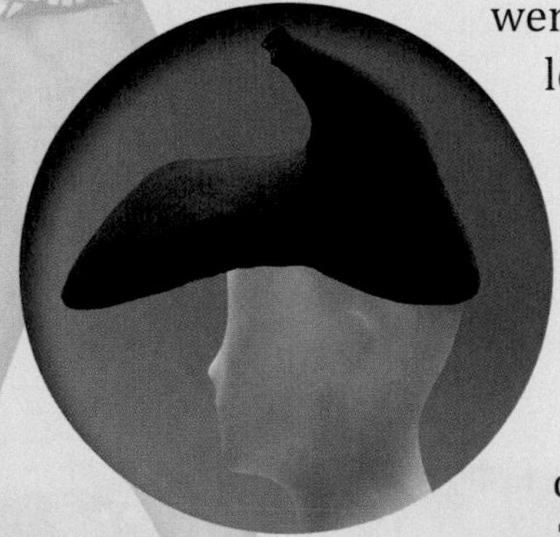

Together, Schiaparelli and Dali created some memorable clothes. Perhaps their most famous creations were the shoe hat and the lobster dress. Dali got the idea for the shoe hat when he put his wife's slipper on his head as a joke. The shoe hat looked exactly like a woman's very large black high heel worn upside down on the head.

The lobster dress was just that. It was a gorgeous full-length gown with a lobster printed on the front. By today's standards, the dress isn't very outrageous. But in the 1930s, it was a head-turning fashion statement.

Get the Look

Of course every stylish woman needs gloves to go with her shoe hat. Schiaparelli's gloves came with fingernails attached to the fingers. You can re-create those famous gloves.

SUPPLIES

- elbow-length satin gloves in whatever color you want
- press-on nails (Go for something wild!)

1. Your gloves probably came with cardboard inserts in them. Leave those inside while you do the project.
2. Follow the directions on your nail set to glue the nails in place over the glove's fingers.
3. Carefully take the cardboard out of the glove. Then do the other one.

Schiaparelli's designs caught the attention of some big Hollywood stars. Celebrities such as Joan Crawford and Greta Garbo were her clients. Mae West had Schiaparelli design clothes for her movies.

Schiaparelli's surreal designs were even worn by one of the most famous women in the world. Wallis Simpson, who later married King Edward of Great Britain, enjoyed Schiaparelli's unusual clothing. Simpson is the person who actually wore Schiaparelli's and Dali's lobster gown.

Get the Look

Make a wild statement like Schiaperelli's and Dali's lobster dress. Be daring or just a bit wacky.

SUPPLIES

- scissors
- 8½ x 11-inch (22 x 28-cm) piece of craft foam
- hot glue gun and glue
- pencil
- paper
- a clean peanut butter jar lid
- wax paper
- fabric paint in a complimentary color to your garment
- a solid colored dress, T-shirt, or jacket

1. Cut the craft foam in half, and glue the two halves together.
2. Sketch or find a picture of a crab, snail, or other interesting creature. The picture needs to be small enough to fit on top of the lid.
3. Trace your picture onto wax paper and cut it out.
4. Place the wax paper shape on the craft foam and trace around it.
5. Cut out the shape through the double-thickness of foam. Glue this foam shape to the outside of the lid.
6. Pour a little fabric paint onto a piece of wax paper. Dunk your stamp into the paint. Stamp the image onto your garment. Be creative and have fun! You could have a whole line of crabs marching up one side.

Since the days of Dali and Schiaparelli, designers have worked surreal ideas into their lines. As you can see, contemporary surreal fashion has come a long way.

In 2008 Viktor & Rolf released ready-to-wear coats that made a statement.

Agatha Ruiz de la Prada debuted a whimsical line of surreal fashion at the 2009 Milan Fashion week.

Modern music stars have taken surreal styles to the extreme. In 2001 Björk wore the now famous swan dress to the Oscars. In 2008 Katy Perry wore Manish Arora's carousel dress. Nicki Minaj is always pushing the limits of fashion. And you can't forget Madonna's cone bra of the 1980s. But Lady Gaga might be the leader of the surreal pack. Her wearable art styles are often shocking, daring, and sometimes hard to look at. In 2010 Lady Gaga wore a dress made of raw meat. She said that dress sent the message that she has rights and is "not a piece of meat."

Next time someone wears a meat dress or a carousel dress, remember that's a 1930s fashion throwback.

WEARING THE PROOF

Fashion trends of the 1920s and 1930s don't just live as memories in Great-Grandma's attic. These looks left a lasting imprint on fashion. No longer are women tightly corseted and covered past the ankles. The flapper dresses of the '20s lifted hems and gave women freedom. The '30s form-fitting gowns celebrated the feminine body.

The '20s and '30s gave women choices in what they wore. And they never looked back. In the decades that followed, fashion designers built on the trends of this era. Fashions in the 1940s and 1950s would continue to merge beauty, fun, comfort, and freedom.

'20S AND '30S LOOKS LEFT A LASTING IMPRINT ON FASHION.

3

COOL CAT

The 1940s and 1950s

In the early 1940s, people across the United States were struggling to rebuild their lives after the Great Depression. Americans turned to music and films as a way to cope with the difficult times, and both influenced the styles of the day.

New trends in music and dance brought about changes in fashion styles. America's youth was jitterbugging to swing music. For many, swing was much more than music—it was a lifestyle. Teens and young adults danced to cool hipster entertainers wearing zoot suits and playing innovative jazz with a pulsing beat.

Swing dancing had women flying in the air and swinging around dance floors. This style of dance was more athletic than styles that came before. As dancing changed, so did clothing. Hems got a little shorter, hovering at the knee. Young women also started wearing fuller skirts with button-down blouses, which allowed for easier movement.

The cute, comfortable skirt and shirt ensembles of swing dancers has definitely not gone out of style. The combo is everywhere from the racks of local department stores to Hollywood's A-list actresses. Eva Mendes, Katie Holmes, and Jennifer Lawrence have all rocked the look.

PUT IT TOGETHER

The 1940s swing look is easy to throw together and is perfect for a summer outing.

Grab a white button-down blouse from your (or your Mom's) closet.

Check the thrift store for a fun, flowy knee-length skirt.

Do a search online for "low-heeled Mary Janes" to find a great pair of toe tappers.

Check an accessory story for a rectangular clutch to finish the look.

SLIPS *and* HOSE

Women in the 1940s changed what they wore under their clothes too. 1940s women began wearing supportive bras and rubberized girdles. Bras and girdles gave them freedom of movement while still slimming and shaping their bodies.

Women also wore slips with fuller skirts over the bra and girdle. Slips helped to protect the modesty of dancers as they flipped in the air.

Stockings were an essential part of women's wardrobes too. Nylon stockings hit the shelves in 1940. They were inexpensive, plus they fit well and looked good. Shops had a terrible time keeping them on shelves. Stockings had a seam along the back. A true lady always made sure her stocking seams were straight along the backs of her legs.

Nylons have fallen out of favor in recent years, but they haven't gone away completely. Catherine, Duchess of Cambridge, is '40s chic. Her famous "buttered leg" stockings honor the past with their sheer, silky, natural sheen. Megan Fox, Mischa Barton, and Hayden Panettiere have been spotted wearing nude-tone hosiery as well.

GOLDEN GLOBE AWARDS
Hollywood Foreign Pr tion
N GLOBE AWARDS
Foreign Press Association
ve on NBC Sunday
ary 13TH 8 EST / 5 PST
N GLOBE AWARDS
Foreign Press Association

MEGAN FOX

Swinging Up-Dos

Dancers couldn't have their hair flying all over. Two hairstyles became the go-to looks in the 1940s. Women either pulled their hair back into a very fashionable chignon or pinned their hair into spit curls.

Chignons are coils of hair arranged around the back of the head. This look was very popular off the dance floor for day or evening styles too. Spit curls were made by wrapping pieces of hair around the finger and using spit to flatten the curl against the head.

Both hairstyles are still popular. Chignons are everywhere on the red carpet. Carrie Underwood, Emma Stone, Jennifer Hudson, and Eva Longoria are just a few of the celebs who've thrown back to the '40s for their looks.

Spit curls are more fun and less elegant than chignons. American Idol contestant Syesha Mercado wore this playful look. Of course, hair spray, not spit, kept her curls in place.

Chignons are everywhere on the red carpet.

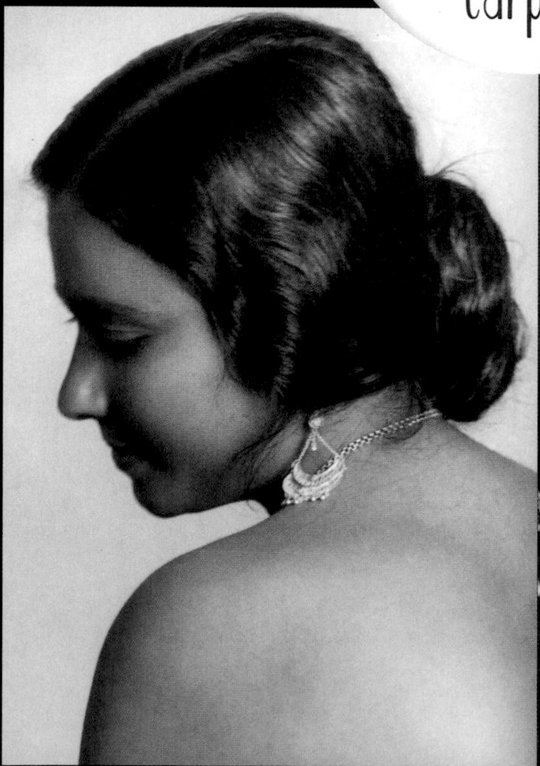

Get the Look

With a little practice, chignons can be a fun way to bring 1940s style into your look.

SUPPLIES

- straight comb
- hot rollers
- elastic band
- 2 side combs
- bobby pins
- hair spray

1. Part your hair loosely on the side.
2. Roll your hair in hot rollers. If you have short bangs, use a curling iron to curl them in the direction of your part.
3. Once the rollers are cool, take them out. Gently comb out the curls, so they aren't little ringlets.
4. Part your hair in front of each ear, so you have three sections of hair. Tie the back section in a low ponytail. Take the left-side section of hair, and twist it toward the back of your head. Secure the hair in place with a side comb or bobby pins. Repeat on the right-side section of hair.
5. Take out the ponytail and divide that hair into three parts. Tie the middle section back into a ponytail.
6. Divide the hair in the ponytail into two sections. Roll one section up and pin in place. Roll the other section down and pin in place.
7. Loosely twist one side section of hair and bring it back toward the rolled hair. Pin the twist in place. Repeat with the other section of loose hair.
8. Use hair spray to keep the hair in place.

From Big Screen to Dinner Tables

Just like today, 1940s audiences were in love with films and the celebrities who starred in them. The styles worn by screen sirens such as Joan Crawford, Lana Turner, and Rita Hayworth represented romance and elegance.

Starlet fashion of the 1940s was driven by American designer Gilbert Adrian. Adrian worked mostly for MGM Studios. His pouf-sleeves, shoulder padding, and other "tricks" could make a less-than-perfect body look perfect. He created the square shouldered look that was prominent in 1940s dresses and skirt suits. Modern-day stars such as Beyoncé, Jessica Alba, and Kim Kardashian keep Adrian's shoulder pad trend alive.

Adrian had a powerful influence on fashion. Women saw his designs on movie starlets and loved them. Department stores began using Adrian's designs to create garments for ordinary women.

In addition to shoulder pads, Adrian also created both the slouch and trench coats and the pillbox hat. His trench coat is still a must-have style. Every star, including Kate Hudson and Anne Hathaway, turn to this timeless trend.

Off the Rack

Coco Chanel created the idea of mix and match separates in the 1930s. But only the very wealthy could afford her couture prices. It was American designer Claire McCardell who created the revolutionary approach of affordable separates. These pieces were sized right "off the rack," or "ready-to-wear" for the general public. This was a groundbreaking idea. Before McCardell's line, clothing was generally made for each individual. Women either sewed their family's apparel or paid a tailor to do it. "Ready-to-wear" clothing was just that. It was ready to wear without additional sewing. This "off the rack" trend is how most people buy their clothes today.

One of McCardell's most famous pieces was the popover dress. This dress was comfortable and trendy. Women loved it. And they still do. Modern versions of the popover are still as popular as ever. Tank dresses with cinched waists are a new take on McCardell's design. Jessica Simpson's clothing line includes several of these modern popovers.

Norman Norell set the trends for ready-to-wear evening apparel. His simple and sophisticated looks gained him attention and respect. Before the 1930s, black was saved for funeral attire. Coco Chanel created a niche for the "little black dress" in the '30s. But Norell made black a popular color for all clothes. His love of black was bold, yet elegant, and appeared in most of his apparel.

One of Norell's lasting designs is the sequined sheath dress. He debuted the look in the early 1940s, and it's a trend that lasts today. Gwyneth Paltrow and Taylor Swift are just a couple of celebs who sparkled on the red carpet wearing this vintage '40s look.

MCCARDELL'S POPOVER DRESS

PUT IT TOGETHER

Pull together a Norell-inspired 1940s evening outfit, and dazzle the night.

Check the prom dress sections of thrift shops for a knee-length sequin sheath dress.

Wear a knee-length wool coat over the dress for a vintage Norell look. Your grandmother might have one of these in her closet.

Grab some simple, low-heeled black pumps. You can find these just about anywhere heels are sold.

Look for nude-colored nylons with a back seam at your local department stores.

THE WAR CHANGES EVERYTHING

In 1941 the United States entered World War II. The war completely changed American lifestyles. As the men went to fight, women were left to take over. Suddenly, women were recruited to do everything from welding aircraft to driving taxi cabs.

The war brought a lot of restrictions to the fashion world. Supplies were rationed or banned altogether. Japan was the main exporter of silk at the time. But Japan was also a U.S. enemy during the war. The government banned all silk items. Leather was reserved for soldiers' leather boots. Zippers and metal buttons almost disappeared. All metals were used to make weapons. The government also rationed fabric. A woman's dress could only use about 3 yards (3 meters) of fabric. That's less fabric than two king-sized pillow cases.

The war forced fashion into a simpler look. For women, the 1940s look featured broad shoulders and a tailored waist tucked into either a pencil or A-line skirt. Hems fell just below the knee.

Pencil skirts with tailored waists are everywhere, even today. You might have one in your closet for special events. And celebs wear them all the time. Selena Gomez and Hayden Panettiere love their pencil skirts.

Top It Off

Hats and hair decorations were the only allowable splurge during the war. Small angled pillbox hats, headbands, snoods, and bows were all the rage. Hats and other decorations are still fun to play with. Accessory stores carry tons of options. Duchess Catherine and other British royalty have been seen in a variety of fun and creative pillbox styles. Kelly Osbourne has rocked the hair bow.

KELLY OSBOURNE

PUT IT TOGETHER

Add a touch of '40s flair to your look by putting on one of these toppers.

Find hair combs, feathers, barrettes, bows, and headbands at accessory stores.

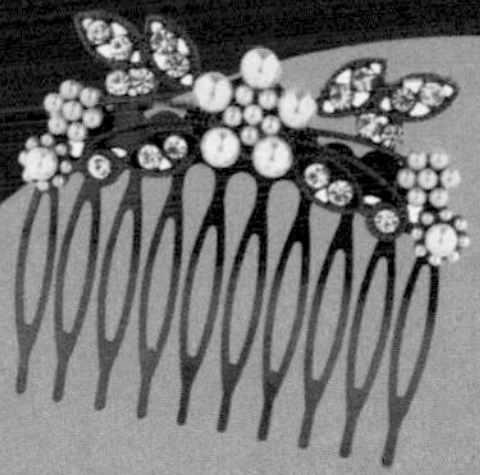

Snoods are crocheted nets that hold the hair back in a stylish way. These are easy to find online.

Make your own pillbox hat or dig through your grandma's attic to see if you can find one.

Get the Look

A pillbox hat is an essential accessory for the 1940s look. Make your own with a little bit of felt and a few stitches.

SUPPLIES

- math compass
- piece of copy paper
- scissors
- sewing pins
- 3 9x12-inch (23x30-centimeter) pieces of felt, all in the same color
- lightweight fusible interfacing
- piece of chalk or a marker
- sewing needle and a spool of thread matching your felt
- 12-inch (30-cm) long piece of ¾-inch (2-cm) wide elastic
- hot glue gun and glue
- silk flowers, netting, or feathers (optional)

1. Draw a circle on a piece of paper with the compass. The circle should be 7 inches (18 cm) across. Cut it out.
2. Pin the paper circle to one of the felt pieces. Using the paper circle as a pattern, cut out a felt circle. Repeat on another piece of felt and on the interfacing.
3. Mark a small "X" on one of the felt circles.
4. Lay the interface circle on top of the felt circle without the "X." Fuse the circles together according to the interfacing's package directions.
5. Lay the second felt circle on top of the interface circle. Keep the "X" side facing up. Sew all the way around the layered circles. Make your stitches as close to the edge as possible. Set the circle aside.

6. Draw two long rectangles on the remaining felt. Each rectangle should be 3 inches (8 cm) high and 20 inches (51 cm) long. Cut the rectangles out. Use one of the felt rectangles as a pattern to cut one out of the interfacing too.
7. Repeat steps 3–5 with the rectangles.
8. Lay the circle on your workspace, "X" side facing up. Pin the long edge of the rectangle around the edges of the circle. Make sure the "X" side of the rectangle faces out.
9. Sew the rectangle to the circle, going all the way around. When you get back to the start, carefully cut off any excess on the rectangle, leaving just ½ inch (1 cm) of fabric. Make a back seam on the hat by sewing the rectangle ends together.
10. Stitch the elastic around the base of the hat. Trim off any extra.
11. Flip the hat inside out.
12. Hot glue decorations to the hat, such as flowers, netting, or feathers.

Creative Footwear

Shoe manufacturers had to get creative during wartime rationing. They developed new looks using natural materials such as cork, flax, straw, and wood instead of leather. Espadrilles made of canvas uppers and rope soles became very much in fashion. Today espadrilles are a summertime must-have for the Hollywood elite such as Jennifer Aniston.

Talented shoe makers such as Italian Salvatore Ferragamo used old furniture pieces for decoration. At the height of the war, Ferragamo's new creations used fishing line and packing string to make surprisingly innovative designs. Ferragamo's funky trends are still with us today. Check any shoe store, and look for shoes with stripes or unusual textures. Or look for wedges or platforms. Those shoes are all throwbacks to Ferragamo creations.

Get the Look

Make your own Ferragamo-inspired shoes for summer fun.

SUPPLIES

- craft knife
- pair of flip-flops
- heavy duty waterproof glue
- solid-color T-shirt
- ruler
- piece of chalk
- scissors
- screwdriver
- clothespins

1. With a craft knife, cut the flip-flop straps off. Leave the "plug" that goes between the toes in place. Be very careful using the craft knife. Always cut away from your body. And don't be afraid to get help from an adult.
2. Glue the toe plug in place.
3. Pop out the two strap plugs on the sides, leaving holes in the sole.
4. Lay the T-shirt out flat. Measure 2 inches (5 cm) up from the bottom hem, and make a chalk mark. Make about 4 more marks at the 2-inch (5-cm) height across the shirtfront. Cut along the marks, through both sides of the shirt. Then repeat the measuring and cutting so you have two 2-inch (5-cm) strips. The strips will be circular. Cut the circles so they are long strips.
5. Tie a knot at one end of one strip. Starting from the sole of the sandal, thread the strip through one plug hole. Use the screwdriver to push it through. The knot should nestle nicely into the hole. Glue the knot in place. Then tie a knot on the other end of the strip. Repeat with the second strip and plug hole.

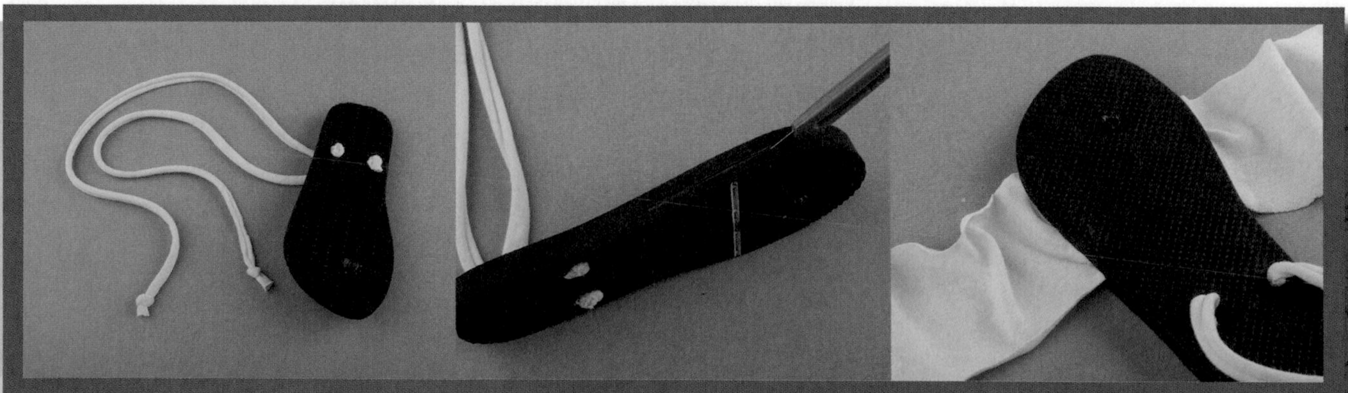

6. Turn the flip-flip sole up. Measure 1 inch (2.5 cm) down from the toe plug, and make a mark. Draw a horizontal line at the mark across the sandal.
7. Cut a horizontal slit that is 3 inches (8 cm) long and 1 inch (2.5 cm) deep on each side of the foam sole. The line you made in step 5 should be at the middle of the slits.
8. Measure 3 inches (8 cm) up from the bottom of the shirt and make a mark. Make about 4 more marks at the 3-inch (8-cm) height across the shirtfront. Cut the strip off through both sides of the shirt. Cut the circle so it's a long strip.
9. Lay the strip out on your workspace. Measure and cut the strip into two 8-inch (20-cm) long pieces.
10. Stuff one end of one 8-inch (20-cm) strip into a side slit. Use a ruler to push the fabric in. Repeat on the other side with the second strip.
11. Glue the strips into the slits. Clamp the strips in place with clothespins while they dry.
12. Wait at least 24 hours for the glue to completely dry before wearing the shoes. When putting on the sandals, tie the toe straps in a bow to fit your feet. Then tie the ankle straps.

Working Women

Throughout American history women had been barred from jobs that paid well or had status. Congress even passed laws that kept married women from getting jobs during the Great Depression of the 1930s. But World War II changed women's place in society. Thousands of American men left to fight in Europe. Women had to keep the factories and other businesses running. By the end of the war, at least 18 million women had joined the work force.

These hardworking ladies were called Rosies. A popular song of the time described "Rosie the Riveter," who worked for victory. Rosies became the symbol of women supporting the American war effort. These women left their popover dresses and heels at home. They tied up their hair and wore dungarees, or denim-pant coveralls, gloves, and protective goggles. The tied up hair and denim look came to represent the proud, hardworking women who still found ways to look pretty.

Get the Look

Hardworking women needed to keep their hair back, but also wanted to look good. The tied head scarf was a popular solution.

SUPPLIES

- a large head scarf

1. Fold the scarf in half diagonally.
2. Hold the scarf behind your head, with the point of the triangle pointing down.
3. Position the scarf under your hair. Pull the two ends up and tie them together on top of your head. Leave the ends loose.
4. Pull the triangle tip up to the top of your head. Stuff all your hair into the pouch.
5. Tie the two ends of the scarf over the triangle point to hold it in place. It may help if a partner holds the point down.
6. Tuck the sides of the scarf in.

MORE MONEY, MORE FASHION

On September 2, 1945, World War II officially ended. It took a while for life to return to normal after the war. After all, 6.2 million employed women left the work force and returned to their roles as wives and stay-at-home mothers. Men came back to the jobs they had left during the war. Even though the wartime rationing of goods had stopped, many goods remained in short supply for many months afterward.

That same year tensions between the United States and the Soviet Union brought the countries into what became known as the Cold War. The United States thought that the Soviets were spying on them. The American government and public grew paranoid. Strict new rules about how to act and what to look like dominated American society during the 1950s. Maintaining a polished appearance became very important. Advertisements showed women cleaning the house in heels and men eating supper in suits. These ads showed how the ideal family should look and behave.

By 1950 the American economy had grown very strong. This economic boom created a new era of prosperity for the United States. For the first time in many years, families had free time and money to spend.

A **Fur** Trend

During the 1950s fur coats became a status symbol for the average woman. Having a mink stole or fox cape gave the impression that a family was successful. Fur became such a symbol of wealth that women wore fur even if they lived in warm places.

Today, fur or faux fur stoles and wraps are still fashionable. A-listers, such as Jennifer Lopez, Paris Hilton, and Mary J. Blige, have all accented their looks with fur.

Fur coats became a status symbol for the average woman.

Get the Look

Get the wealthy 1950s fur stole look without breaking the bank.

SUPPLIES

- 1¾ yards (1.6 m) faux fur
- pins
- sewing needle and a spool of thread matching your fur color
- a thimble

1. Fold the faux fur lengthwise with the fur facing inside. Pin the long sides in place, leaving both ends open.
2. Sew along the long end so you end up with a long tube. Use the thimble to protect your thumb. The fur will be thick.
3. Refold the tube so the seam is in the center. Pin one short end together and sew it closed.
4. Put your hand inside the tube through the open end. Carefully pull the sewed end out to turn the stole right-side out.
5. Pin the open end closed and sew it shut. Use small stitches that camouflage well under the fur.

Dior's New Look

After the war women wanted to indulge their fashionable side. Fashion designer Christian Dior celebrated this new attitude with his "New Look." Dior created garments that defined excess. Some of his dresses featured calf-length crinoline skirts that used up to 80 yards (73 m) of fabric. That much fabric could almost cover a football field.

Dior's look took the fashion world by storm. After the boxy, plain looks of World War II, his creations were refreshing. However, the New Look required that women wear a girdle and cinch their waists with a corset. Dior's designs featured the hourglass figure—a large bosom, tiny waist, and full hips. For the correct effect, his full skirts required stiffened bodices and slip petticoats.

Waists in the 1950s were astonishingly small. Today's trendsetters don't wear waists quite so tight. But the 1950s full skirt and cinched waists are still popular. Zooey Deschanel and Emma Watson have both twirled this look on the red carpet.

ZOOEY DESCHANEL

For day wear ladies also loved Dior's S-Line. Dior's S-Line was a sculpted hobble two-piece skirt suit. Hobble skirts are very similar to pencil skirts, but the hem is mid-calf and the slit in the back is very small or non-existent. Hobble skirts got their name from the restrictive way it makes a woman move.

Hobble skirts aren't the most comfortable fashion, but they are a lasting one. Solange Knowles and Anne Hathaway have pulled this look off. In 2011 the Chanel brand brought back the hobble skirt in some creative ways too.

Women accessorized the hourglass waist and S-Line looks with cute hats, gloves, and spiked stiletto heels. A pearl necklace with matching clip-on earrings and a coordinated handbag finished the look.

PUT IT TOGETHER

This fun, sophisticated outfit is perfect for a school dance or just a fancy evening with friends.

Look for a dress with a fitted bodice and flared skirt at your local department store.

Check your grandma's closet for a vintage 1950s handbag. Or find a rectangle-shaped bag at an accessory store.

Accessory stores carry gloves and pearl necklace and earring sets to polish off your outfit.

Browse your local shoe stores for spiked heels to compliment your dress.

Balenciaga's Timeless Trends

BALENCIAGA SACK DRESS

Designer Cristóbal Balenciaga also shaped the fashion trends of the 1950s. The Spaniard's imaginative creations are timeless trends you can see in your closet even today. Balenciaga's sack dress was loose fitting and hung straight from the shoulder to the knee. His bolero was a cropped open jacket inspired by the matador's traditional suit. Balenciaga's seven-eighths length sleeve was created so women could show off their watches and bracelets.

The sack dress is a wardrobe staple even now. These comfy, stylish dresses are worn by everyone from Reese Witherspoon to Vanessa Hudgens.

Get the Look

In the 1950s eyeglasses and sunglasses became accessories. Designers created pointed and winged frames that were especially popular. You can make your own cat-eye glasses to get the retro look.

SUPPLIES

- pencil
- ruler
- unlined paper
- scissors
- 1 pair black wayfarer sunglasses
- 4-inch (10-cm) square piece of faux leather in your choice of color
- a permanent marker in a color matching the faux leather
- hot glue gun and glue

1. Draw a 1-inch high by ¾-inch wide (2.5x2-cm) crescent shape on the paper. Cut out the shape. Then write an "L" on it.
2. Hold the shape to the left eyepiece on the sunglasses. The top and bottom points of the crescent should match up with the outside shape of the glasses. Trim the shape to fit, if needed.
3. Flip the crescent shape over, and trace it on your paper. Cut the shape out. Draw an "R" on this shape.
4. Place your paper patterns on the leather. Trace around the patterns with the marker.
5. Cut out the leather pieces.
6. Glue the leather pieces on the sunglasses. If you wish, embellish the leather with beads. Let the glue dry before wearing your sweet shades.

THE RISE OF TEEN FASHION

At school young men and women were expected to follow a strict dress code. Full circle skirts influenced by Dior with starched crinoline petticoats and sweater sets were typically worn by girls. Girls were often forbidden to wear pants.

But outside of school, teens began to rebel. For the first time in history, teens started dressing less like their parents and more like pop culture celebrities. Two things brought celeb styles to 1950s teens—TV and rock 'n' roll.

The invention of TV made a huge impact on style. TV showed viewers what was happening around the world. They saw the newest Parisian fashions on the *Today Show*. They watched their favorite singers belt out songs. And for the first time, people saw commercials for apparel and cosmetics—and they bought what was advertised to them. Sound familiar?

In 1951 DJ Alan Freed debuted his show, *Moondog Rock 'n' Roll Party*, spinning pop rhythm and blues music. Freed introduced rock and roll sounds to radio listeners. The sounds of rock and roll were life-changing for teens. So beloved was the new American music scene that youth fashion worldwide was influenced by it. In America rock and roll was the sound of rebellion and independence.

Many of the new rock and roll stars, including Elvis Presley, sported a unique look. They wore a variation of the zoot suit paired with the look of a "greaser." Zoot suits were made famous by jazz musicians in the '30s and '40s. These suits combined high-waisted trousers with baggy jackets. The term "greaser" comes from the greasy look that hair gel gave a guy's hair.

TYPICAL 1950S SCHOOL OUTFIT

Get the Look

The classic black and white saddle shoes that school girls wore are a must-have 1950s look.

SUPPLIES

- a pair of clean white canvas tennis shoes with laces
- a black fabric marker
- a can of acrylic gloss spray

1. Remove the laces from the shoes, and set them aside.
2. Use the marker to draw an outline on one side of a shoe, following the stitch lines that go along the toe and heel areas. Then color in the section. Repeat on the other side. Don't color the tongue, toe, heel, or sole of the shoe.
3. Repeat step 2 on the second shoe.
4. Spray the shoes lightly with an acrylic gloss spray.
5. Let the shoes dry for 24 hours before lacing and wearing them.

JAMES DEAN

ZAC EFRON

This look showed the world they didn't follow the rules.

Several stars took the greaser look to another level. They paired their gelled hair with crumpled T-shirts, leather jackets, and jeans. This look showed the world they didn't follow the rules of dressing and acting like society wanted them to. Stars including Marlon Brando in the movie *The Wild One* and James Dean in *Rebel Without a Cause* didn't want boundaries. They, and many teenagers, wanted the freedom to dress and act however they wanted. Some people called these rebels "hoods," short for hoodlum or outlaw.

The "hood" look is a classic 1950s style. Teens danced to rock and roll wearing sneakers and rolled-up blue jeans. Today the look is as popular as it was then. Katie Holmes, Kate Hudson, Selena Gomez, and Vanessa Hudgens have all pulled off the dungaree look with '50s inspired boyfriend jeans. Zac Efron, Chace Crawford, and Taylor Lautner have been photographed with the ever popular rebel chic T-shirt and leather jacket.

PUT IT TOGETHER

The hood look is a timeless and very comfy look. You might just be able to pull an outfit together from pieces you already own.

Turn your favorite pair of jeans into '50s style. Just fold the pant legs into cuffs that fall just above your ankles.

Hit up the thrift store to find a long-sleeve plaid shirt. Roll up the sleeves for a retro look.

Ask your grandma if she has any short scarves. Tie one off to the side of your neck to really polish off the look.

Penny loafers were a huge 1950s trend. If you can't find those, loafers in fun colors or even simple flats will work just fine.

Jazz singer Billie Holiday made the hair flower famous in the '30s and '40s. It was still a popular accessory in the 1950s. You can find them at any accessory store.

Get the Look

During the 1950s Americans went crazy for poodles. Poodles were so popular that images of them appeared on everything from playing cards to skirts. Make a poodle skirt, and pair it with a polo shirt and saddle shoes, to really bring back the '50s.

SUPPLIES

- 48-inch (122-cm) square of felt, your choice of color
- measuring tape
- a piece of chalk or a marker
- fabric scissors
- 1 package iron-on Velcro
- 7-inch (18-cm) square of black or white felt
- hot glue gun and glue
- 25 inches (64 cm) of ¼-inch (.6-cm) wide ribbon, your choice of color
- 1 plastic googly eye

1. Lay the large felt square flat on a cutting surface. Fold the left edge over to the right edge. Then fold the top edge down to the bottom edge to create a 24-inch (61-cm) square.
2. Draw a curved line from the top left corner to the bottom right corner. Cut along that line. Unfold the felt.
3. Fold the felt into a half circle with folded edge on top. Then, fold the left side over the right side.
4. Measure 4 inches (10 cm) from the left side corner across the top fold and make a mark. Then measure 4 inches (10 cm) from the top corner down the left-side fold and make another mark. Draw a rounded line to connect the marks. Cut along the line to make a waist hole.
5. Open the skirt into a circle again. Cut a straight line from the bottom of the skirt to the waist hole.
6. Cut two 2-inch (5-cm) long pieces of Velcro.

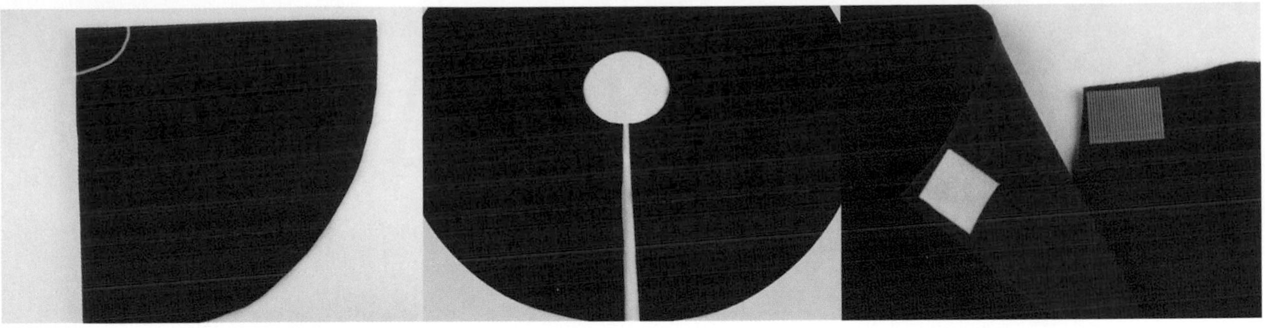

7. Try on the skirt and mark where the ends meet to comfortably fit your waist. Follow the directions on the Velcro package to apply one piece of Velcro on the outside of the skirt and the other on the inside matching your mark.
8. Find a poodle printable online and print it. Cut out the printable. Lay the poodle pattern on the square of felt and trace it. Cut the poodle out of the felt.
9. Make a mark on the skirt where you want the middle of the poodle to go. Hot glue one end of the ribbon to the mark. Continue gluing the ribbon up the skirt, adding loops in the ribbon as you go. Tuck the ribbon over the waistband and glue in place.
10. Glue the poodle over the ribbon on the dot you made. Then glue on the dog's googly eye.

GETTING ACTIVE

As middle class families had more money and time for traveling, people wanted more casual clothes to wear for their "down time." Continuing her success into the '50s, Claire McCardell started designing relaxed leisure and sportswear. These casual fashions moved away from the "high society" and well-to-do prices of the Paris and New York runways. People didn't need to pay expensive designer prices for their leisure wear. Once again, McCardell's fashions were available in department stores in a variety of reasonable prices for all budgets.

Designers experimented with fabrics to make comfortable, fun clothing for the new active lifestyles. They used stretch fabrics, bright colors, florals, plaids, and animal prints. Women enjoyed playsuits, beach dresses, and cover-ups. McCardell marketed summer wear separates that included coordinating sleeveless sun tops, skirts, and shorts. Aloha shirts became quite a fad for men. Collared polo-style shirts and Bermuda shorts also became fashionable.

People wanted more casual clothes to wear for their "down time."

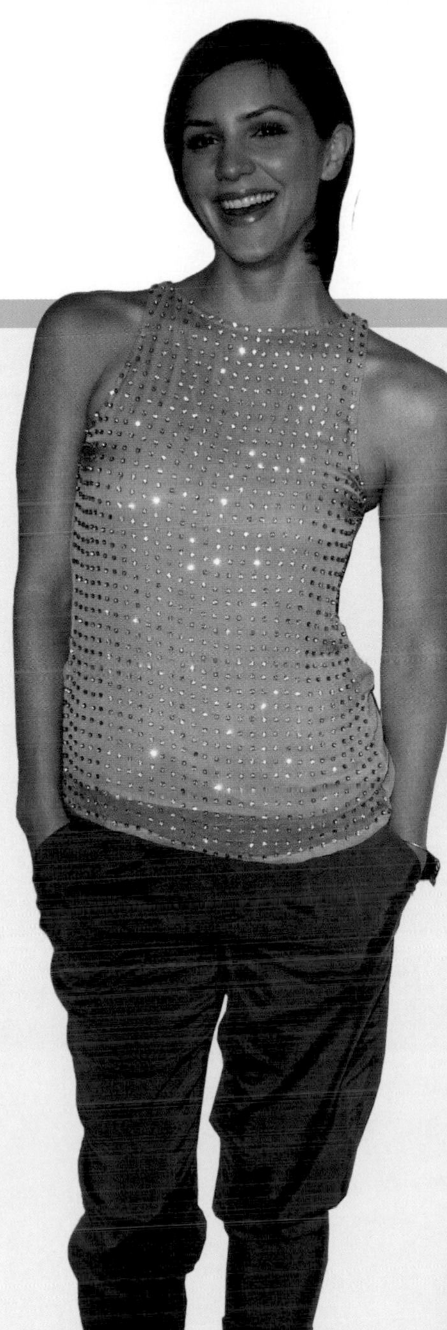

KATHARINE MCPHEE

The trends found in today's beachwear are obvious throwbacks to the 1950s. Clothing stores everywhere sell Bermuda shorts and polo shirts. McCardell's sleeveless sun tops are today's tanks.

KATY PERRY

And what's summer without bright colors and Aloha shirts and dresses?

Sporty Styles

During wartime women didn't just keep the factories going. They were recruited to keep sports fans entertained too. These athletes led the way to many groundbreaking styles that are still with us today.

1943

More than 500 women were recruited to play pro baseball for the All-American Girls Baseball League. Players wore baseball caps, jerseys, and cute short skirts. They were also required to wear lipstick and nail polish to keep their ladylike look.

1946

Louis Réard invented the bikini. The garment's name came from the Bikini Atoll, a nuclear testing site in the South Pacific. It was named for the "explosive" effect it had on anyone looking at it. Too skimpy for women at that time, it remained unpopular until the '50s.

Of course, this style is hot today. Tabloid mags are always snapping shots of A-listers in their tiny bikinis.

1948

Swim champion and movie star Esther Williams partnered with Cole of California company. They introduced bathing suits made of Lastex, a revolutionary fabric made of rubber and nylon. Lastex made suits lightweight and fast drying. Before this time suits were made of cotton or wool.

Actress Bridget Bardot helped promote a more modest bikini. The charming floral print covered to the waist and was more like shorts with a cropped tank top.

The high-waisted bikini is making a comeback. Taylor Swift, Bella Thorne, and Ke$ha have all taken a dip in this retro fashion.

1953

early 1950s

Teenage girls began to dominate the sport of cheerleading. Before World War II, cheerleading was very popular with young men. Female cheerleaders adopted mid-calf length skirts worn with letterman sweaters and saddle shoes. As the years went on, cheerleading skirts have gotten shorter and more versatile. But they are still throwbacks to the first ones worn in the 1950s.

HAIR *and* MAKEUP

Before the 1940s American women didn't use many cosmetics. Most women simply washed with soap and water then applied cold cream and white powder to their faces. But beginning in the 1940s, primping and the artistic application of cosmetics helped women express themselves. Sweet smelling perfumes, pancake makeup, and lipstick became popular, everyday tools to make women look and feel their best. It was during this time that the fantasy of the "bombshell" was born.

The term "bombshell" originated in the '30s from the platinum haired, red-lipped beauty Jean Harlow. Harlow starred in a movie called *Bombshell*. She was dazzling and flirty—so the name stuck around. By World War II the meaning expanded to redheads and brunettes. These bombshells typically flaunted an hourglass figure, fresh faces, and a lipsticked smile.

JEAN HARLOW

The Ultimate Bombshell

You can't talk about "bombshell" actresses without mentioning the most iconic one of them all—Marilyn Monroe. Monroe wasn't just a 1950s film star. She has become one of the most legendary style icons in the world.

Countless actresses have imitated Monroe's classic look. Scarlett Johansson, Gwen Stefani, and Katherine Heigl have all shown their curves in body-hugging gowns and accented their smiles with bold red lips. Lady Gaga, Madonna, and Christina Aguilera have imitated Monroe's platinum blonde locks.

Monroe wore many memorable dresses. The white pleated halter dress that blew around her in *The Seven Year Itch* sold for $5.6 million at an auction in 2011. Then there's the skin-tight nude-color sequined dress she wore when singing "Happy Birthday" to President John F. Kennedy. She was quite literally sewn into that dress. And countless stars have followed in her fashion footsteps.

But possibly Monroe's biggest fashion contribution wasn't what she wore, but how she wore it. Monroe was daring and scandalous in her day. She knew she was beautiful, and she flaunted it.

Monroe's glamorous style is enduring and timeless. Need proof? Macy's carries a junior clothing line dedicated entirely to her. The store even has a version of the white halter dress. Britney Spears called on Monroe's classic style for her Onyx Hotel Tour, wearing white blonde hair, deep red lips, and diamonds. Even Paris Hilton has worn the classic Marilyn look on the red carpet.

THE LIST GOES ON AND ON ...

Makeup Explosion

Women needed products to get that bombshell look. Lipstick was the first product to really fly off the shelves. By the beginning of the 1940s, ladies applied lipstick more than they brushed their teeth!

During the '40s teens wore the lipstick pout, copying stars such as Rita Hayworth and Veronica Lake. The lipstick pout accentuated the lips. Fashionista Joan Crawford was known to apply lipstick past her natural lip lines, doubling their size.

Actresses of the time also wore greasepaint created by Max Factor. Factor made flexible greasepaint in a wide range of shades that helped make actresses look more natural in close-ups for film. These greasepaints were called pancake makeup. The thick, oily cream, applied with a sponge, covered acne, freckles, and scars, creating a flawless complexion. The actresses looked so stunning that women everywhere were asking for the makeup too. The products became available to the public in the late 1930s. And by the 1950s they were in widespread, everyday use. Today liquid and powder foundation have replaced greasepaint. The products may have changed, but the goal of flawless complexions is still the same.

Women in the 1950s wore their brows thick and generously penciled in. The feline, or cat eye, became a staple in eye makeup, swooping toward the temple and enlarging the look of the eye using a brow pencil. Eye shadows also started to be produced at this time. By the late 1950s every woman was influenced by Audrey Hepburn's dark doe eyes that were shadowed, lined, and plumped with mascara.

The cat eye and doe eye looks are still popular today. Nicole Scherzinger and Kim Kardashian have both flashed cat eyes. Emmy Rossum and Katy Perry are just two of the countless celebs who keep the doe eye look going.

AUDREY HEPBURN
1956

Get the Look

Give your makeup routine a boost of retro with the doe eye look.

SUPPLIES

- shimmery, light-colored eye shadow
- darker eye shadow, complimenting the lighter one
- black eyeliner pencil or liquid liner
- eyelash curler
- black mascara

1. Apply light colored eye shadow on both eyelids. Also lightly apply it on both sides of the bridge of your nose.
2. Apply a darker shadow in the creases of your eyelids.
3. Underline the lower lashes with an unbroken line of eyeliner.
4. Curl your lashes. Then apply two coats of mascara. Make sure it doesn't get clumpy.

EMMY ROSSUM
2013

Timeless Tresses

The most popular hairstyle of the '40s was the "peek-a-boo" cut made popular by actress Veronica Lake. The sultry hairdo fell just past the shoulders and covered one eye. Women everywhere started wearing this simple look. But it was impractical for factory workers who kept getting their hair caught in machinery.

The U.S. government's war department actually asked Lake to style her hair differently for the safety of workers!

Many stars still wear the timeless, gorgeous peek-a-boo style. Julianne Moore and Jennifer Lawrence are just two people who've blown viewers away with this simply lovely look.

VERONICA LAKE

Get the Look

A major hair trend in the '50s was the greaser pompadour hair style. The pompadour is particularly hot right now for both men and women. Jenny McCarthy, P!nk, and Rihanna have all shown off this high-flying style.

SUPPLIES

- thin spaced comb with a thin rat-tail end
- claw clip
- bobby pins
- hair spray

1. Make a part on the top of your head in a horseshoe shape. Clip the hair on top of the head with a claw clip.
2. Twist the rest of your hair in the back into a simple bun. Use bobby pins to pin it in place.
3. Unclip the hair at the top of your head and lay it back over the bun.
4. Use the rat-tail end of the comb to grab a 1-inch (2.5-cm) section of hair from the front. Hold the hair straight out from the head. Starting at the middle point of the hair section, comb down the hair toward your head. This will tease the roots into more height. When you're done, leave the hair hanging down over your face.
5. Grab another 1-inch (2.5-cm) section of hair from behind the first section. Tease that hair.
6. Repeat teasing the hair in sections until you have done all the hair that isn't in the bun.
7. Carefully lift the teased hair up and lay it back on the head. Gently comb the teased hair back to smooth it out.
8. Pin the ends of the hair around the bun in the back.
9. Spray with hair spray to set the style.

A TURNING POINT

Some fashion historians consider the 1940s and 1950s a turning point in style and culture. In those two decades, Americans defined who they were as a nation and evolved a style that is still prevalent today. The fashion of those decades changed not only how people dressed, but how society viewed beauty.

The trends that would shock in the 1960s and 1970s were deeply influenced by styles invented in the '40s and '50s. And teens' rebellion agaist wearing clothes like their parents would lead to a culture of rebelliousness in the decades to come.

WHAT WAS OLD IS NEW AGAIN!

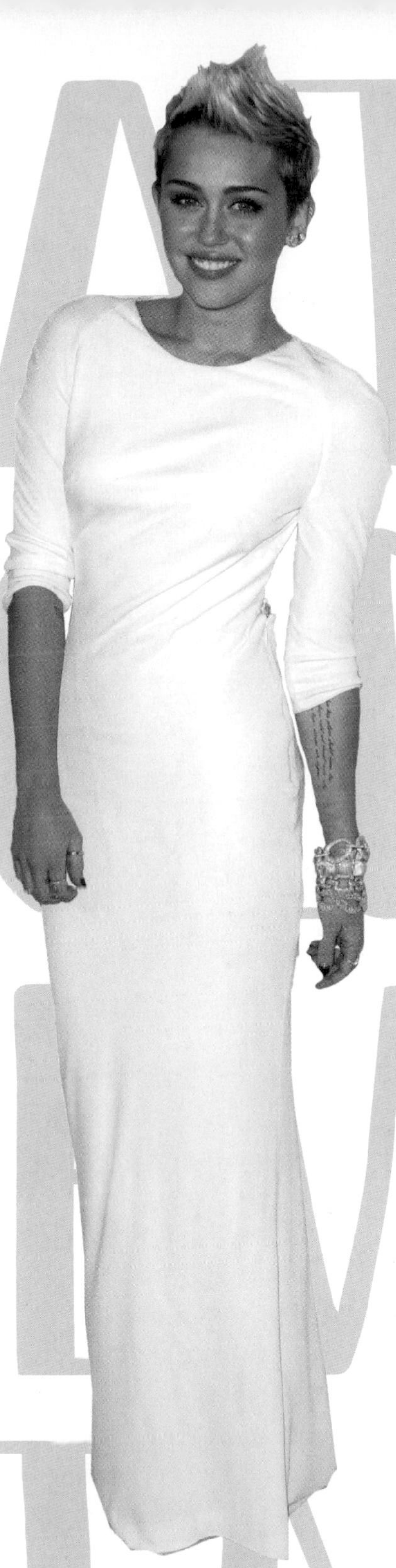

4

Far Out

The 1960s and 1970s

By the 1960s and 1970s, designers in England and the United States started to influence how women dressed. They increasingly drew their inspiration from everyday people with a certain style or flair. Designers looked to stylish young women who wanted to break free from the past. More youthful fashion options allowed younger people more room for personal expression and rebellion.

From year to year, styles changed so fast even the most fashionable women struggled to keep up.

In November 1960 John F. Kennedy became the youngest man ever elected president of the United States. The next year he and his family moved into the White House. Almost immediately, Americans became fascinated with the young and glamorous Kennedys. They were especially drawn toward the president's wife, Jacqueline, who was often called Jackie. She was refined, beautiful, and most of all, stylish.

Raised in a wealthy family, the first lady had a flawless taste in fashion and a classic style. Before her husband's presidential win, she often bought her clothes from the finest fashion houses of Europe. After his election, however, Jackie turned to American designers to show her support for U.S. businesses.

PUT IT TOGETHER

In the early 1960s, movie star Audrey Hepburn, like Jackie Kennedy, had enormous influence in the fashion world. Stars such as Anne Hathaway and Natalie Portman have imitated Hepburn's famous look from the movie *Breakfast at Tiffany's* (1961) in recent fashion magazines. You too can re-create the style with items you probably already own.

Take a plain, sleeveless black dress.

Add a chunky beaded necklace.

Style your hair into an updo.

Wear a pointed black heal.

To take the look to the extreme, put a comb decorated with fake diamonds in your hair, pull on a pair of long black gloves, or wear large, round-brimmed sunglasses.

New Style

ANNE HATHAWAY

Jackie asked French-born American designer Oleg Cassini to help her establish an individual style. Together they created the first lady's new look. Inspired by several European designers, he dressed Jackie in shift dresses. These sleeveless garments hung straight from the shoulders without a defined waist. Cassini also favored A-line shift dresses with skirts that slightly widened at the base.

Some fashion journalists did not approve of this new style. They said the A-line shift dress was shapeless. They called it "the sack." But American women instantly loved this modern, elegant look. Shift dresses were easy to wear and flattered many different figures. Shift dresses never went out of style. Today modern celebrities Gwyneth Paltrow, Jennifer Anniston, and Anne Hathaway have been spotted wearing this timeless look.

Another fashion trend Kennedy popularized was the pillbox hat—a small brimless round hat with a flat crown and narrow sides. She famously wore a pillbox to her husband's presidential inauguration. Lady Gaga, Kate Middleton, and Paris Hilton are just a few of today's celebrities who have been seen wearing pillbox hats.

Long after she was first lady, Jackie remained a fashion trendsetter. But she is best remembered for the simple and chic look she made popular in the early 1960s. Even today, Jackie's look is considered the height of classic American style.

Get the Look

Scarves were a trademark Jackie Kennedy accessory. To copy Jackie's signature style, look for boldly patterned scarves in a discount store or vintage shop.

USING A SQUARE SCARF

1. Fold the scarf diagonally to make a triangle shape.
2. Place it over your head, with the middle tip in the back, and tie the two remaining ends under your chin.

USING A LONG RECTANGULAR SCARF

1. Fold a colorful, long scarf into a headband.
2. Tie it at the back of your head under your hair.
3. Pull the knot to one side so that the ends of the scarf dangle over your shoulder.
4. Add sunglasses to complete the look.

Animal **Print**

Leopard prints were all the rage.

Among sophisticated women in the 1960s, leopard prints were all the rage. Coats and hats in faux leopard fur were very popular. Leopard skin patterns also appeared on just about every accessory, including purses, scarves, gloves, and jewelry.

In recent years, leopard and other animal prints have made a comeback. As animal print fans such as Sarah Jessica Parker, Mary-Kate Olsen, and Ashley Argota know, a little leopard print can make a look seem both retro and current.

Get the Look

Try adding leopard print fabric to an accessory you already own.

SUPPLIES

- leopard print fabric
- handbag or wallet
- scissors
- fabric glue or tape

1. Measure the area of your handbag or wallet that you want to cover in leopard print.
2. Cut the leopard print fabric to size.
3. Glue or tape the fabric onto your handbag or wallet.

YOUTHQUAKE

Mary Quant opened a clothing shop in London, England, in 1955. She wanted the boutique, named Bazaar, to appeal to young, working women and students. Quant sensed they wanted something different—clothes that were fun, easy to wear, and most of all youthful. After taking a few sewing classes, Quant started designing clothes for her store. Working out of her home, she cut and sewed cloth into simple flared dresses.

The colors she used were not the pastels popular at the time. Rather, she favored the bright and bold, such as tomato red and mustard yellow. But the most unusual thing about her dresses and skirts were the hemlines. Other designer dresses fell at the knee or below. Quant's hems were inches higher, hitting the mid-thigh. Quant's higher hems sent a lightning bolt through the fashion industry. Her simple change helped create the miniskirt.

Get the Look

Flower designs were everywhere in the 1960s. You can add a little flower power to your wardrobe by making a 1960s-style flower appliqué.

SUPPLIES

- 2 pieces of felt of different colors
- scissors
- fabric glue
- sewing supplies or pin

1. Cut a simple flower shape with five rounded pedals out of a piece of felt.
2. Cut out a felt circle and sew or glue it to the flower's center. Be sure to use different colors for the flower and the circle—the wilder the contrast the better. For instance, try combining hot pink with lime green or neon blue with bright orange.
3. Sew or pin your appliqué to anything you want to decorate from a plain shirt to a jacket to a purse.

Swinging **London**

Quant's miniskirts and minidresses were an immediate sensation. Other London designers soon followed her lead. They created clothes to sell in boutiques for the younger generation. In the past designers looked to the fashion houses of Paris for inspiration. But these English designers wanted to break away from tradition. They began to create unique, inexpensive, ready-to-wear clothing. This new style of "Swinging London" spread fast.

At the same time many American teenagers rebelled against their parents. They wanted more freedom. Miniskirts and other new fashions, such as hip huggers and headbands, gave these teens a new way of expressing themselves.

Many adults disapproved of these new trends. But in time, even older women began wearing London-inspired fashions. The magazine *Vogue* declared that the entire fashion industry had experienced a "youthquake."

Miniskirts got shorter and shorter. The most extreme were microminis. Micromini hems rose as much as 8 inches (20 centimeters) above the knee. Women paired microminis with tights in order to move freely without showing their undergarments. They also accessorized with Mary Jane styled square-toed shoes with low, blocky heels.

Miniskirts were probably the most enduring fashion trend of this era. The once-shocking miniskirt has been a fashion go-to for generations. Today, nearly every female star—from Lea Michele to Gwyneth Paltrow to Jennifer Aniston—enjoys donning a miniskirt.

PUT IT TOGETHER

With just a few accessories, you can turn a minidress into a complete Swinging London look.

minidress

colorful or patterned tights

large dangling earrings made from bright colored plastic

low heeled pumps

plastic handbag

large sunglasses with bright yellow, orange, or green frames

anything decorated with the British "Union Jack" flag

TWIGGY

Many fashionable women looked to London models for style tips. The most popular of all was Twiggy. Discovered when she was only 16, Twiggy was a new type of model. For one thing, she was average height, but very thin. Previously, models were expected to be elegant, tall, and curvy. With her tiny frame and short haircut, Twiggy looked more like a boy than a stylish woman. Yet she became one of the world's first supermodels. Women everywhere copied her look. Twiggy began the trend toward super-skinny models that continues today.

Get the Look

Twiggy, was named the "Look of 1966." A key part of this style was her heavy, black lashes. Actresses such as Ginnifer Goodwin have re-created this vintage makeup trend for the red carpet. With a few simple steps, you can get this dramatic look too.

SUPPLIES

- nude lipstick
- black mascara
- false eyelashes

1. Put on a nude lipstick or even leave your lips bare.
2. Add layers of long false eyelashes to your lids.
3. Use mascara to paint long lower lashes on the skin below your eyes.
4. If you don't want to put on fake eyelashes, fill out both your upper and lower eyelashes with black mascara.

GINNIFER GOODWIN

New **Colors** and Patterns

The mid-1960s also saw big changes in fashion's use of color and pattern. Outfits often featured bold blocks of color. Frequently, eye-catching color combinations, such pink and orange or green and yellow were paired together. Years before, such color combinations had been seen as jarring. Now they seemed modern and exciting. For instance, color blocking was the hottest spring trend of 2011 and continues today. Famous designers such as Jil Sander, Marc Jacobs, and Dries Van Noten offer collections with bold, contrasting bursts of color. Some modern celebrity color blockers include Carey Mulligan and Emma Stone.

Colorful swirling patterns and kaleidoscopic prints were also embraced in the 1960s. Many garments were adorned with bold rings of color created through tie-dyeing. Inspired by designs from India, fabrics featuring paisley prints were also popular. Paisley prints have highly detailed curved and feather-like patterns.

The designer most remembered for his powerful use of colorful geometric patterns was Emilio Pucci. The famous Pucci prints have made his 1960s designs popular items for vintage shoppers. Fergie, Julia Roberts, and Jennifer Lopez are just a few of the celebrity Pucci collectors. From time to time, 1960s-style color combinations and powerful patterns come back in style.

Get the Look

One of the most popular fashion fads of the late 1960s and early 1970s was tie-dyeing. Ask an adult to help you use this dyeing method to transform a white cotton T-shirt into a crazy rainbow of color.

SUPPLIES

- new white T-shirt
- reactive dyes in squirt bottles (available from a crafts store)
- rubber bands
- plastic gloves
- garbage bags
- plastic wrap
- scissors

1. Wash and dry a new white T-shirt.
2. Pinch up about 3 inches (8 cm) of fabric and tie it at the bottom with a rubber band. Repeat until there is no more fabric to pinch.
3. Put on plastic gloves and spread garbage bags on your workspace. (Also, be sure to wear old clothes that you can throw out if they get splattered.)
4. Squirt the colored dyes in a random pattern until the shirt is covered in dye.

5. Cover the shirt with plastic wrap, and let it sit overnight.
6. Unwrap the shirt. Use scissors to cut the rubber bands.
7. Hand wash the shirt in cold water to remove excess dye.
8. Wash the shirt by itself three times in hot water in a washing machine, and then dry it.

TAKING IT TO EXTREMES

DISC DRESS

As the 1960s wore on, many followers of fashion wanted the same thing—something new. Many hoped to be the first to discover the next fad. This sense of adventure encouraged designers to try out all kinds of strange ideas.

Some of their boldest experiments were in the materials they used. Sewing a dress from thread and fabric suddenly seemed old-fashioned. Designer Paco Rabanne, for instance, created a minidress out of plastic discs. Using pliers, he "sewed" them together with metal rings.

Rabanne's famous disc dress was uncomfortable, but wearable. Other designers went to even further extremes. Emmanuel Ungaro made an evening gown from Ping-Pong balls. Betsey Johnson created a dress out of plant fibers stuffed with seeds. If you watered the dress, seedlings would grow out it. Lady Gaga has not let the world forget that different and unusual materials can be used to make a fashion statement. She has worn dresses made from Kermit the Frog dolls and raw meat.

Get the Look

Let the extreme styles of the 1960s inspire you. Try making a necklace with unusual materials from a hardware or craft store.

SUPPLIES

- washers or nuts
- ribbon
- fake flower or another decoration

1. Measure an area around your neck the length you'd like your necklace to be.
2. Cut the ribbon to size.
3. String a few bolts or washers on the ribbon.
4. Add a fake flower or another decoration to give the necklace a little more flair.
5. Tie the ends of your necklace together around your neck.

A more practical material that inspired many designers was polyvinyl chloride, or PVC. This is a type of plastic. A piece of cloth covered with PVC looked shiny and wet. PVC was used to make skirts, dresses, and handbags. But it was most frequently seen on raincoats. By making them waterproof, the plastic on these garments was both useful and fashionable. Pop stars such as Christina Aguilera, Rihanna, and Katy Perry have all worn outfits made of PVC.

Of all the unusual materials used in 1960s fashion, the most popular was paper. Scott Paper Company made the first paper minidresses. As a promotion, it offered its customers the dress for just $1.25. When more than half a million women bought one, the fashion industry took notice. Soon department stores and boutiques were selling complete lines of paper dresses.

Paper minidresses were usually sleeveless with a slightly flared skirt. Often they were printed with bold designs of stripes, zigzags, or animal prints. Sometimes the paper was left blank, so women could color in their own designs. With just a pair of scissors, women could easily alter the hemlines and make their paper dresses as short as they dared.

Paper dresses fell apart after just a few uses. But that's what was so fun about them. It was hard to get bored with your wardrobe when you were always throwing away one dress and buying a new one.

Some fashion experts predicted that in the future all clothing lines would be made from paper. The paper dress craze, however, quickly faded. The dresses were too impractical and uncomfortable to stand the test of time.

PAPER DRESS
1967

Get the Look

Sixties-style paper dresses are hardly practical, but they are fun and easy to make.

SUPPLIES

- patterned wrapping paper
- poster board or cardboard to use as a pattern
- pencil
- scissors
- colored duct tape

1. Cut a pattern that can be used for both the front and back of the dress. Try lying down and having a friend trace the shape of your body on the poster board or cardboard. Make it wide enough to cover the sides of your body also. The top should be sleeveless with a slightly scooped neck. The skirt should flare out from the waist, and the bottom should hit a few inches above the knee.
2. Trace the pattern onto the wrapping paper. Cut out two pieces—one for your front side and one for your backside.
3. Hold the two pieces together around your chest to make sure the dress will fit. Tape the two sides together.

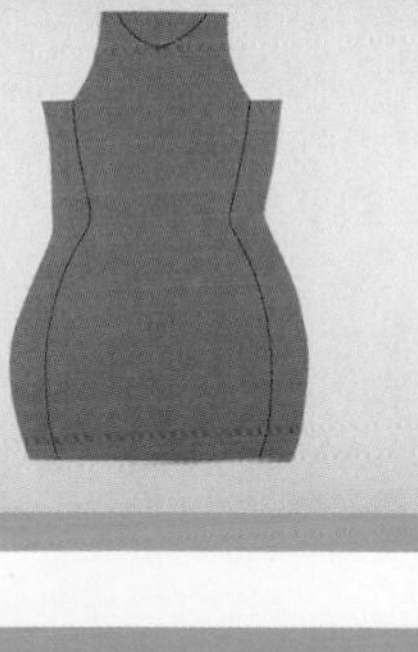

Hairstyles

African-American women once felt pressured to use harsh chemicals to straighten their hair. But as fashion rules were broken in the 1960s, many decided to let their hair grow naturally. Some women embraced the afro, a style recently sported by singers Beyoncé and Esperanza Spalding. Styled by combing hair straight from the scalp, the afro created a ball of hair all around the head. During the 1960s and 1970s, women often paired afros with gold hoop earrings, the bigger the better. If you have kinky or curly hair, you might want to try experimenting with natural hairstyles. Even if your hair is naturally straight, a pair of gold hoops can give your look a retro feel.

ESPERANZA SPALDING

Get the Look

Girl groups such as the Ronettes helped make this big hairstyle, called the beehive, popular in the 1960s.

SUPPLIES

- curling iron
- comb or brush
- bobby pins

1. Curl the front of your hair with a curling iron.
2. Backcomb your hair by combing it backward toward the scalp.
3. Part your hair at the front on one side and pull out one section in the front.
4. Brush the rest of your hair to one side.
5. Pin it up with bobby pins.
6. Gather hair into a ponytail.
7. Twist the ponytail around itself, and secure with bobby pins onto rest of hair.
8. Pull the front section of hair around to the back of head and secure with bobby pins.

HIPPIE STYLE

As many social and political changes occurred in the 1960s, the hippie movement swept across the United States. Hippies were young people who wanted to live freer lives than their parents. They did not want to obey society's rules about how people should behave. Hippies often chose not to get a job or get married, as their parents expected them to do.

Many hippies also opposed the Vietnam War. America's involvement in this conflict divided the nation. The military action and loss of U.S. soldiers' lives spurred protests among American youths. This activism spread to the civil rights movement. Hippies organized marches, sit-ins, and protests.

In short, the hippies valued love over money, peace over war, and the natural over the unnatural. And they had the courage to make their opinions known.

Hippie fashion was seen on the streets as well as TV and movies. Hippies of both sexes grew their hair long and straight. They did not style it. They also wore blue jeans and beaded necklaces called "love beads." Many female hippies rejected the still popular miniskirt. They instead favored the maxi—a long flowing dress with a hem that reached the floor. They often paired maxi dresses with simple sandals or just bare feet. Their new fashions allowed them to express their ideas of peace and love.

Get the Look

Style your hair the hippie way: Dry and comb your hair so that it's super straight with a middle part. Adorn your simple do with something from nature.

SUPPLIES

- a chain of small wild flowers worn as a headband
- a large flower tucked behind your ear
- a feather clip at each temple

Old and New

Hippies did not care for artificial fabrics favored by some designers. Instead, they preferred clothing made of natural fibers, especially cotton. They also refused to spend much money on clothes. Instead of shopping in department stores and boutiques, hippies dressed in a combination of old and new clothing from secondhand shops. At the time, most Americans did not want to be seen wearing used clothes. But to the hippies, it was a way of showing the world that they did not care about money or expensive things. It showed that they were going against the established norms of the time.

Thrift store shopping also allowed hippies to dress in their own creative way. Unlike other fashionable people, hippies did not dress based on current styles. They wanted to decide for themselves what looked good.

From secondhand stores, hippies purchased antique lace petticoats and velvet jackets or flowing satin gowns from the 1930s. They also bought vintage brooches and buckles. Hippies shopped in inexpensive import stores too. There they bought clothing from around the world. Favorite items included cotton skirts from India, jackets from China, and robes from Morocco.

PUT IT TOGETHER

Creating a hippie look is fun and easy.

Pair a T shirt with a floor-length cotton skirt.

Put on a velvet jacket.

Add a string or two of plastic beads, a floppy hat, and casual, low-heeled sandals.

Wear your hair down and loose, or, if its long enough, in two braids.

Jeans and T-shirts

Hippies' love of blue jeans and T-shirts as a means to identify with the working class made an important contribution to fashion. Both of these clothing items already had a long history. For more than 100 years, men working strenuous jobs wore jeans because they were so durable. For many decades, men had also worn T-shirts as underwear. But by the mid-1970s, these special uses were forgotten. In casual settings a T-shirt and jeans became almost a uniform for both men and women. Some modern celebrity jeans and T-shirt wearers include Megan Fox, Tallulah Riley, and Emma Watson.

Hippies also expressed themselves by customizing their clothing. They often made an item one-of-a-kind with embroidered designs, patches, or appliqués. Many people also knitted or crocheted hats and other garments. Handcrafted items were much more special than anything you could buy in a store.

Not all young people were hippies in the '60s and '70s. But nearly everyone—young and old—was affected by hippie style. Designers and clothing manufacturers started making clothes that mimicked what hippies wore. Many people who had no interest in this movement were still impacted by its fashion.

Get the Look

In the early 1970s, denim—the fabric used to make jeans—was king. There were denim hats, denim bags, denim coats, and denim jackets. Denim jean jackets have since become a fashion staple found in many women's wardrobes. Demi Lovato and Jessica Alba are just a couple of today's celebrities who enjoy wearing denim jackets.

SUPPLIES

- denim jacket
- patches and buttons
- fabric tape or glue

1. Tape or glue patches of colorful fabric over any rips and tears.
2. Add buttons with slogans and images you like. (Look especially for buttons with a peace sign or a yellow smiley face—two of the most popular images from the period.)

In the early 1970s, people preferred faded jeans with wide flared legs known as bell-bottoms. Modern wearers of wide-legged pants include Heidi Klum, Katie Holmes, and Kourtney Kardashian. Today, however, fashion-conscious people prefer skinny jeans in a dark color.

Some Americans still love wearing flared jeans as much as they did decades ago. Similarly, T-shirts printed with patterns, slogans, and logos remain a popular garment for people of all ages, including young stars Dakota Fanning, Kendall Jenner, and Emma Roberts.

Americans still love wearing flared jeans as much as they did decades ago.

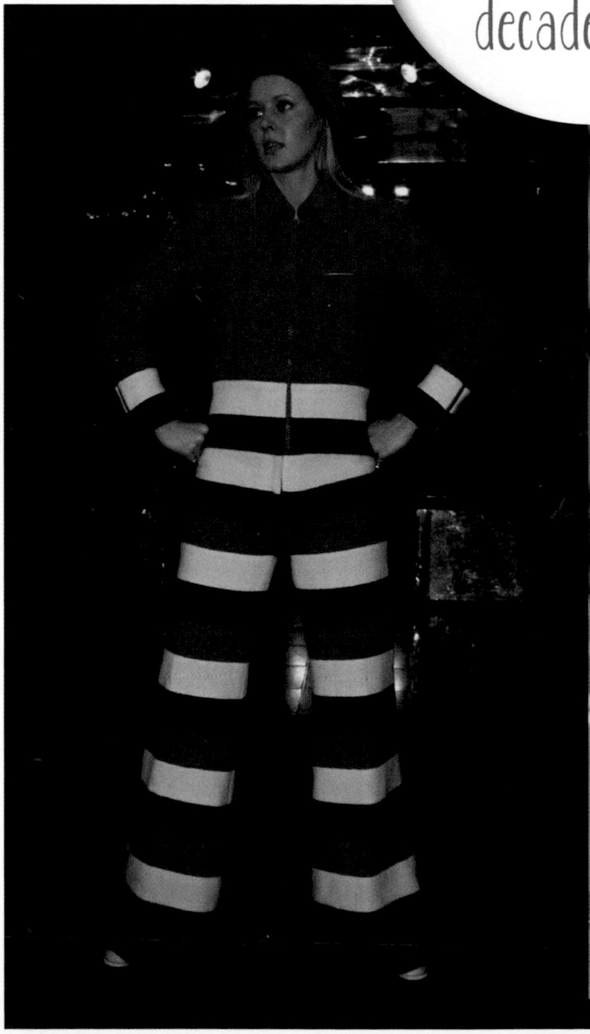

Get the Look

Young people in the late 1960s and early 1970s turned their old jeans into flares. You can make your own flares from a worn pair of straight-legged jeans.

SUPPLIES

- pair of jeans
- piece of cloth
- scissors
- sewing materials

1. Open up the jean leg by cutting along the outside seam of each leg from the hem to the knee.
2. Measure the leg opening you just made. Then cut two triangles from a piece of cloth. (For real 1970s style, use cloth with a wild pattern or bold color.) The length from the point to the base of the triangles should be the same length as the cuts you made in the jeans.
3. Sew the triangles into the slits in both legs to create a new pair of flares.

GLAM, DISCO, AND PUNK

Rock and pop music have long had an influence on the fashion world. For instance, music fans copied the style of singer Elvis Presley in the 1950s and the rock band the Beatles in the 1960s. But in the 1970s, the link between popular music and fashion grew even stronger. Musical acts such as David Bowie and Blondie merged music and fashion as performance art. Many of the biggest fashion trendsetters today—from Katy Perry to Gwen Stefani to Lady Gaga—are stars of pop music.

BLONDIE

GWEN STEFANI

Get the Look

Throughout the 1970s, rock concerts were a big business. Fans gathered in huge arenas to watch their favorite bands perform live. As a souvenir, they often bought T-shirts sold at the shows decorated with the band's name or the cover art of their latest album. Wearing a vintage band T-shirt is an easy way to add a little 1970s style to an outfit. T-shirts from the 1970s are hard to come by and often expensive. But new versions of old shirts are now produced by many online vendors. For a real 1970s vibe, look for shirts celebrating bands such as the Rolling Stones, Led Zeppelin, the Grateful Dead, and the Ramones. Modern celebrities Kristen Stewart, Jessica Alba, and Rachel Bilson have all been spotted in band T-shirts.

Glam Rock

One of the most outrageous musical and fashion styles of the 1970s was glam. Glam rock was particularly popular in England. Its biggest stars included David Bowie, Lou Reed, and Grace Jones. Glam rockers were known for their extreme performance costumes. Many of their outfits could be worn by males or females. They were made from shiny fabrics in bold and metallic colors and often covered with glitter or rhinestones.

PUT IT TOGETHER

For glam rock stars, the more outrageous their clothes were, the better. Add a little glam into your style.

a plain T-shirt under a fur or metallic vest

a pair of skinny jeans or satin leggings

feather boa to accessorize

A trademark of glam rockers, for both males and females, was wearing heavy, colorful makeup on their eyes and cheeks. David Bowie was particularly known for his elaborate eye makeup. At the time a man wearing makeup was considered extremely daring. Even so, some die-hard fans, both men and women, copied this look.

DAVID BOWIE

Get the Look

Glam rock was also called glitter rock for good reason. The elaborate stage makeup of glam stars was all about bright colors and glittery shine.

SUPPLIES

- several different colors of glittery eye shadow
- eye shadow brush

1. Apply silver or gold eye shadow to you eyelid and below your eyebrow.
2. Top it with a few different bold colors of glitter shadow. A typical glam combination would be purple on the edge, pink in the middle, and yellow on the inside of the eye.
3. Add streaks of bright red blush to your cheekbones.

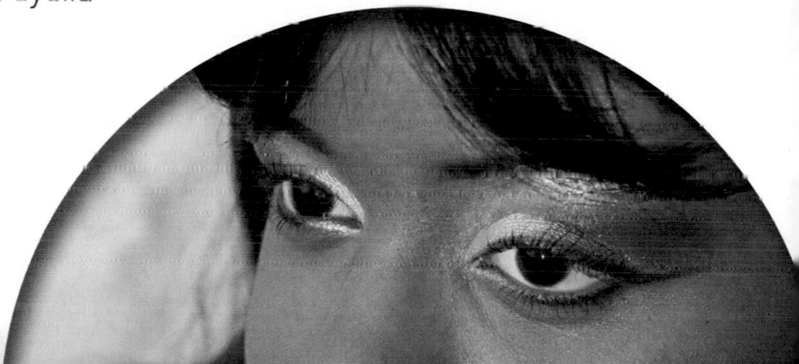

At the Disco

By the mid-1970s, glam rock's popularity was fading. Then disco, dance music with a strong beat, started taking over the airwaves. Movie stars and celebrities gathered at Studio 54, a nightclub in New York City. They were often dressed in fashions made just for the disco scene. Young people everywhere copied their looks at their own local discos.

At discos a mirrored ball sent pulses of light over the dancers as they moved. Disco wear had a shine and shimmer that reflected the light.

The typical disco dress was sleeveless with narrow shoulder straps. It hugged the body at the top but flowed outward at the bottom. Disco dresses were usually paired with very high heeled sandals, often in silver or gold. Versions of the disco dress can still be seen in dance clubs today.

Another popular disco look was a satin jumpsuit with a halter top. "Queen of Disco" Donna Summer is remembered for dresses covered in sequins or glitter.

DONNA SUMMER

Men also had their own disco outfits. They usually featured tight pants and colorful shirts with the top buttons undone to show off several heavy gold necklaces. The most famous disco look was worn by actor John Travolta in the movie *Saturday Night Fever* (1977). His all-white suit with an unbuttoned black shirt is one of the most famous movie costumes of all time.

Shiny silver disco-style dresses have also recently been spotted on many celebrities, including Selena Gomez and Jessica Simpson. One of Katy Perry's most famous looks was a minidress that looked like it was made from a disco ball.

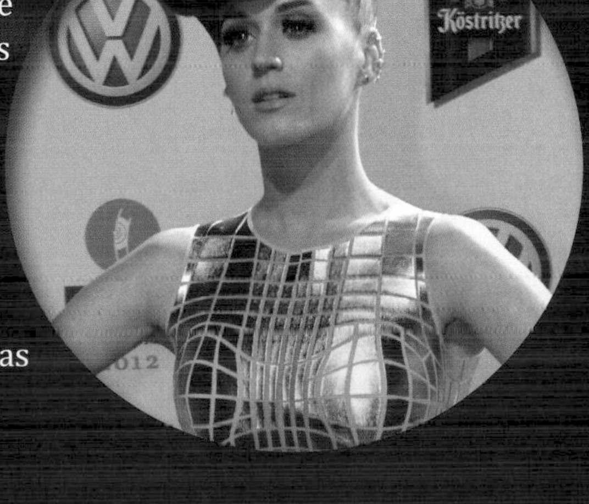

Punk

No one had more scorn for disco than the fans of punk music. Punk musicians, such as the Ramones and the Sex Pistols, did not like the slick sound of disco or other pop music. They liked music that was simple and rough.

Punk fashion was also raw and rowdy. Punks' favorite color was black. They often wore black sweaters, trousers, and jackets with matching shoes or boots. Females dressed in leather skirts, sometimes paired with fishnet tights.

Punks were also known for their anti-fashion hairstyle. Both men and women styled their hair into mohawks, dying it bright, jolting shades.

Female punks used makeup to rebel against how people wanted women to look. Women were expected to wear makeup to look pretty. Punks instead used it to make themselves look unique and a little bit frightening. Punks often sported lots of black makeup around their eyes. They even colored their lips with black lipstick.

Punk was a very extreme style. But it has endured through time. Miley Cyrus, Avril Lavigne, and Kelly Osbourne are just a few of the many celebrities who have added punk elements to their personal style.

PUT IT TOGETHER

As long as you have plenty of black in your closet, donning a '70s punk look is simple.

Start with a black T-shirt, black or plaid skirt, and tights.

Add black low boots with a chunky heal.

Finish up with black nail polish, black eyeliner, and a few streaks of sprayable temporary hair color in a bold, bright hue.

If there's a tear in your shirt or a rip in your tights, fasten it together with a few large safety pins—the favorite "accessory" of 1970s-era punks.

DRESS FOR SUCCESS

During the 1970s, many women had become tired of constantly changing fashions. They also felt that the fashion industry was failing to create the kinds of outfits they needed most. These women did not want to look like teenagers, hippies, or rock stars. They wanted beautiful clothes that made them look like sophisticated, adult women.

Working women were particularly frustrated. Many women in the United States then supported the Women's Rights Movement. This movement sought equal rights for women. Among these was the right to hold good, high-paying careers. Throughout the 1970s, women flooded into careers that had before been off-limits to them. Many of these women had never worked outside the home. In the workplace, they desperately wanted to prove themselves and earn the respect of their bosses and coworkers. Part of that effort was dressing as though they were serious and responsible professionals.

The miniskirt, for instance, suddenly seemed too revealing for the workplace. Clothing makers started experimenting with lower hemlines. The new midi came down to the mid-calf, while the maxi stretched all the way down to the floor. Neither the midi nor maxi skirt totally caught on with the public. In fact, some women cut slits in these low-hemmed skirts because they thought they were too old-fashioned.

CARMEN ELECTRA VENUS WILLIAMS

Soon the fashion industry presented women with another choice—pants. One of the first designers to embrace women's pants was Yves Saint Laurent. He created an elegant tuxedo suit for women in 1966. The suit was supposed to replace an evening gown. But many people found the idea of pants on a woman in a formal setting to be shocking. Even prominent and famous women were kicked out of restaurants and theaters if they insisted on wearing Saint Laurent's tuxedo suit or pants.

Just a few years later, it became common for women to wear pantsuits to work or public events. Pantsuits were made up of a top or jacket with a matching pair of trousers. Hillary Clinton became famous for her pantsuits during her 2008 run to become president and continued the trend during her time as Secretary of State.

PUT IT TOGETHER

In 1977 fashion designer Ralph Lauren created clothes for the title character of the movie *Annie Hall* and started a fashion fad. You can make your own Annie Hall style by visiting the men's department of a thrift store. Be sure to pick pieces that are just a little big on you, but that don't overwhelm your frame.

men's khaki pants

white, button-up shirt

black vest

blue necktie with white polka dots

black wool felt hat

GLORIA VANDERBILT

Also in the 1970s, designer jeans came into fashion. Jeans had long been worn by young women, but always in a casual setting. Designer jeans were now seen as an elegant clothing item appropriate for a night on the town.

Calvin Klein and Gloria Vanderbilt were two of the biggest names in designer jeans. Their jeans were cut slim and usually dyed dark blue or black. They also displayed the designers' logos on their back pockets. Designer jeans were fairly expensive, costing at least two or three times as much as regular pairs of blue jeans. Women wanted to show off the logos so everyone would know they could afford such a costly and trendy item.

Other designers set out to satisfy women's desire for comfortable, practical clothing. Geoffrey Beene and Halston, for instance, began creating flowing clothing made out of jersey knit. This soft fabric allowed women to move much more freely. Another fan of jersey was designer Diane Von Furstenberg. In 1973 she introduced the wrap around dress, which hugged the body and tied at the waist. This easy-to-wear style became an instant classic. Von Furstenberg still offers her loyal customers dozens of new wrap dresses each season. Kate Middleton and Beyoncé are just a couple of the many modern wearers of the wrap dress.

Get the Look

One of the most famous hairstyles of the 1970s was the Farrah Flip. It was named after Farrah Fawcett, an actress who starred in the TV hit *Charlie's Angels* (1976–1981). If you have bangs and a layered cut, you can do a modern take on Fawcett's popular look.

SUPPLIES

- curling iron or flat iron

1. Part your hair in the middle or on one side.
2. Use a flat iron or curling iron to flip your bangs away from your face.
3. Separate a layer of hair on each side of your head near your cheekbones.
4. Use the flat iron again to flip each layer into a gentle backward curl.

Separates

In the 1970s many American designers also began producing fewer dresses and more separates. Separates are tops and bottoms that can be worn in different mix-and-match combinations. This modern American style of dressing is still embraced by elegant stars such as Kerry Washington and Katie Holmes.

Since the 1970s this style has spread to other countries, putting American designers and American fashion in the international spotlight. To this day American designers and American style still have enormous influence over international fashion.

PUT IT TOGETHER

The 1970s are often remembered for their wildest fashions. But toward the end of the decade, one trend was all about restraint. Halston and other 1970s designers began creating outfits with each piece of clothing in the same neutral color, such as white, cream, or gray. You can re-create this classic look by dressing in one color from head to toe.

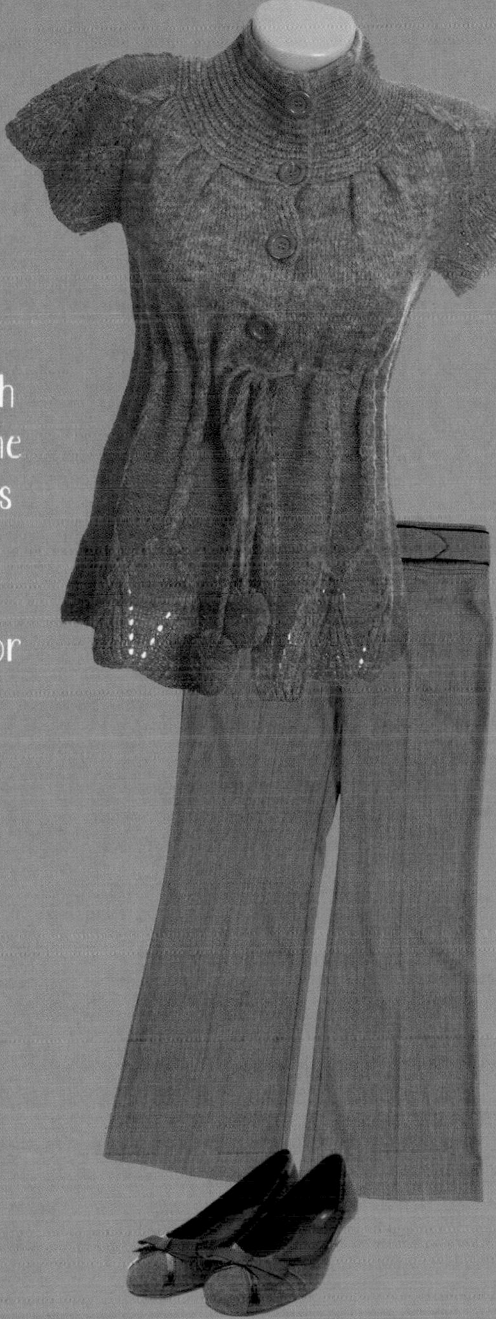

plain white or gray shirt

white or gray slacks

simple white or gray shoes

DARING TO BE DIFFERENT

In the fashion world, the 1960s and 1970s were a time of rapid change. No period before or since saw as many fashions come in and out of style. Plenty of hot trends from that era were abandoned for new and daring looks. Space Age goggles and paper dresses have never made a comeback. But other fashions have endured. Designer blue jeans, pants for women, and miniskirts are styles that are unlikely to ever go away. Many other trends, such as paisley patterns and go-go boots, turn up on runways every few years.

The era's biggest influence on today's fashion was not a garment or a color or a pattern, but an attitude. This period in history invited fashionable women to break the rules and experiment with fashion, and wear it proudly. Today that attitude is essential as you search for your own personal style. Trendsetters in the 1960s and 1970s dared to be different. They led the way for the big, bold fashion of the 1980s and the carefree, casual styles of the 1990s.

THESE TWO DECADES WERE AN EXCITING, DAZZLING TIME

5

Prepped and Punked

The 1980s and 1990s

The 1960s and 1970s had been a time of rebellion and protest. By the beginning of the 1980s, people were ready for more stability. Americans became more concerned about working hard and making money. They also needed a break from the realities of work and money. Many people found it in the form of princesses and pirates.

In September 1980, the world met a shy preschool teacher named Lady Diana Spencer. Shy Di, as she was called, was engaged to marry Prince Charles of Great Britain, who would someday be king.

The real-life prince and princess were all over magazine covers in the months leading up to their July 1981 wedding. On that day 750 million people worldwide watched Diana become Princess of Wales. Her fairy-tale dress, designed by David and Elizabeth Emmanuel, became a sensation. Its train was 25 feet (7.6 meters), the longest on record for a British royal wedding. It featured large puffed sleeves and a silk taffeta skirt placed over a tulle petticoat.

Diana's wedding dress is the ultimate example of '80s fashion: large, dramatic, and romantic. But Diana became a style icon beyond her wedding dress. After her wedding, *Vogue* magazine's fashion editor Anna Harvey advised Diana on her clothing. They determined what the then future Queen of England should wear.

New *Princess*

Diana often took fashion risks. Today, Britain's newest princess, Duchess Catherine, continues to set fashion trends. Like Diana, Catherine caught the world's attention when she married Prince William, son of Charles and Diana. Some of Duchess Catherine's fashion trends include the use of nude colored heels and wearing modestly priced clothing from mainstream shops. When Catherine wears a dress, it sells out in stores soon afterward.

Get the Look

Diana famously wore an emerald and diamond choker that the queen had given her. Except Diana wore it on her forehead as a headband rather than around her neck. Create your own fairy-tale look by taking a traditional piece of jewelry and finding a new use for it.

SUPPLIES

- an old choker necklace
- bobby pins

1. Find a choker necklace in your jewelry box.
2. Measure it around your forehead for size.
3. Fasten it just below your hairline with bobby pins.
4. Now you have a ready-made headband fit for a fashionable princess.

Thar Be '80s Pirates Ahead, Matey

Part of the new romantic fashion of the 1980s included the pirate look, started by London designer Vivienne Westwood. Quirky 1980s performers such as Pat Benatar, Adam Ant, and Boy George used wild hair and makeup to set Westwood's high fashion couture to music. They wore lacey shirts under velvet jackets, tight black pants, and unruly hair. These fashionable followers of Westwood's '80s trend might just as easily been mistaken for Captain Hook. Modern-day pirates can take their cues from stars such as Johnny Depp, Russell Brand, and Helena Bonham Carter, who rock haphazard styles mixed with glam. Lots of disheveled layers, over-the-top accessories, and at least one long, skinny scarf complete the look.

Part of Vivienne Westwood's '80s style was a rejection of her earlier '70s punk designs. A few of these trends carried into the '80s, with torn clothes, T-shirts sporting rebellious slogans, and shredded denim remain popular. P!nk, Gwen Stefani, and Avril Lavigne have let punk influence both their music and their fashion.

PAT BENATAR

GWEN STEFANI

PUT IT TOGETHER

Whether you choose to be a pirate or a punk, your style is sure to draw attention. To rock the full punk look, you will need these essential pieces.

Find a tank top in a bright neon color. Yellows, greens, and oranges look great.

Pair your top with a mismatched bottom. For instance, you may choose striped, leopard print, or even plaid pants or a skirt.

Your footwear should be military-style boots.

To complete that tough punk look, you will need a leather belt with spikes or studs.

Dressing for Political Power

The world of '80s politics took a very different turn from punk and pirate fashion. Ronald Reagan, a former actor, was elected president in November 1980. His conservative policies helped to grow private businesses. Programs that helped the poor were cut back. His politics matched the change in attitude at the time.

Following his wife Nancy's example, people began buying flashier clothes from designer labels. The first lady hosted lavish balls for her Hollywood friends. Showing off your financial success with how you dressed was expected.

Americans became more image-conscious. They spent large amounts of money on the designer names and logos that became popular in the 1980s.

Even Margaret Thatcher, Britain's prime minister throughout the 1980s, brought her own style to the decade. Thatcher wore stiffly sprayed "helmet hair" and skirts with suit jackets. She proved that a woman could be feminine and in charge at the same time.

Women's suit styles have changed since the '80s. However, many women including Halle Berry still follow the "suit is power" model.

A woman could be feminine and in charge at the same time.

NANCY REAGAN

MARGARET THATCHER

HALLE BERRY
The Hollywood Reporter
L'ORÉAL
PARIS

Nancy Reagan and Margaret Thatcher modeled the trend of power dressing. Power dressing was a style of clothing that made its wearers look more skilled and confident. Influential women in the United States began dressing like these popular role models. This look included power suits and large, wide shoulder pads.

A popular 1988 film, *Working Girl,* showed the power of a woman in a suit. A secretary's idea is stolen by her boss. To steal her idea back, the secretary dresses in more powerful-looking attire. Her new power suits and shoulder pads end up helping her career.

This shift in women's fashion was rooted in the fight for equal rights. For many decades, most women working outside the home in businesses were secretaries. The '80s brought women into leadership roles. To be taken seriously, women needed to dress powerfully. This often meant dressing like a man. Shoulder pads gave women a wider-shouldered silhouette. A female executive's suit jacket looked like one a man would wear.

Get the Look

Any shirt or dress can go from now to '80s shoulder pad wow by simply including two pieces of fabric and all the filling you can handle.

SUPPLIES

- large piece of fabric
- measuring tape
- scissors
- sewing materials

1. To get the size of fabric you will need to make your shoulder pad, measure your shirt from neckline to shoulder seam and subtract 1 inch (2.5 centimeters).
2. Make a circle with a diameter of that size, meaning if your seam measures 9 inches (22.5 cm), make an 8-inch (20-cm) circle.
3. Fold the circle of fabric in half, filling it with stuffing or batting.
4. Sew the open sides closed.
5. Tack one end of your shoulder pad near the shoulder seam and the second end near the neck seam.
6. Repeat these steps for the other side of your shirt.
7. Prepare to stun with your commanding shoulder pad presence.

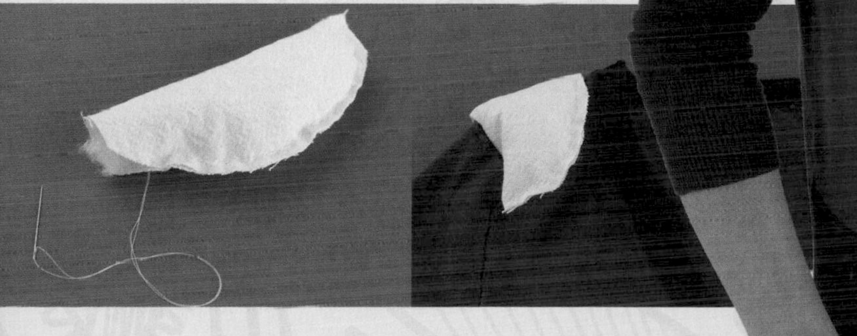

'80s Fashion Goes Prime Time

In the early '80s prime-time royalty ruled the most dramatic looks. Nighttime TV soap operas such as *Dynasty* and *Dallas* featured powerful female characters. The costumes on these shows were very feminine in all their Hollywood glamour.

Many women of the '80s mirrored the dramatic appearances of *Dallas* and *Dynasty's* stars. Women's bold colored makeup, take-charge clothing, and big hair showed their confidence. Celebrities of today, including Heidi Klum, have followed this trend. They use bright makeup, elaborate hairstyles, and dramatic, over-the-top styles to show their self-assurance.

Get the Look

Big hair was all the rage in the 1980s. The bigger, the better. Characters Krystle and Alexis famously feuded on *Dynasty*, even pulling each other's hair. But none of that fighting could mess up their 'do. They followed two essential '80s rules for big hair—hair spray and teasing.

SUPPLIES

- comb
- hair pick
- strong-hold hair spray

1. To tease your hair, take a 2-inch (5-cm) wide strip of hair and lift it straight up.
2. With your other hand, comb the hair closest to your head backward toward the roots. Tease your hair slowly to avoid tangles.
3. Repeat this process over the crown of your head.
4. Lift sections of hair at the roots with a pick and spray heavily.
5. Spray the whole head to cover. If it holds up in front of a fan, you know you are soap opera ready.

Designer Fashion **Loves** the **Yuppies**

Yuppies loved making money and buying expensive things.

One of the most popular terms to come out of the 1980s was the word *yuppie*. Yuppie stands for Young Upwardly Mobile Professional. *Yuppie* is used to describe the 1980s ideal and the style that went along with it. Yuppies valued hard work and individual responsibility. They also loved making money and buying many expensive things, such as Rolex watches and designer bags. They wore leather, fur, and brand names on their clothing. Designers knew these professionals made enough money to afford their designs.

Yuppies loved to accessorize. Their earrings were famous for being huge. Many were large, plastic designs made with primary colors. They were also geometric shapes like circles, squares, and triangles with polka dots, stripes, or other patterns. For the 2013 Academy Awards, Halle Berry wore drop pendant black onyx and diamond circle earrings to go with her striped Versace gown. Huge geometric patterned earrings, especially featuring large dangles, are favored by Kelly Osbourne, Beyoncé, and the Kardashian sisters among others.

PUT IT TOGETHER

To get that Yuppie "causal cool," look for the three Ps–pastels, pearls, and pairs.

Find clothes in light pastels, like blues, purples, and especially pinks or peaches. White and khaki will also work well paired with '80s pastel.

Grab a long strand of pearls.

Pair your pastel Yuppie cardigan sweater with its perfectly matched pastel shell underneath. Drape your cardigan over your shoulders, tying the arms loosely over the front just below your collarbone.

Pair your pastel sweater combo and pearls with a khaki or white skirt. Finish the look with plain flats. White, black, or '80s powder pink will do.

GOING '80S TO THE MAX

Fashion of the 1980s had its extremes. While there were the yuppies, there were also pop stars like Madonna wearing street styles. As many dressed up to impress, many also dressed down in sporty styles that came from the gym.

Get the Look

One major hair trend of the '80s was the side-pony. To go, like totally '80s, put that side-pony as high on your head as you can. It's radical.

SUPPLIES

- comb or brush
- ponytail holder

Pull your hair tightly to one side. Make sure there are no bumps as all your hair should look evenly smooth in the ponytail.

Preppies and Valley Girls

Preppy style came from casual sportswear attire associated with "prep" schools and prestigious colleges. But students kept this fashion long after graduation. They wanted to show everyone they would be successful in life, so they dressed the part. Required for every preppy's wardrobe was the Izod Lacoste alligator polo shirt. To imitate the '80s preppy look, push your collar straight up. Preppies also wore kilt skirts, cashmere, twin set cardigans, and tweed jackets.

In 1981 the hit movie *Chariots of Fire* was released. It helped make V-neck cricket sweaters a popular part of preppy attire.

A much-parodied look of the 1980s was the Valley Girl. These girls were from the San Fernando Valley near Los Angeles. They were typically wealthy and obsessed with clothing and shopping. Valley Girls put the California spin on being a yuppie. Valley Girls wore short, swinging skirts, stripes, leg warmers, and headbands.

PUT IT TOGETHER

Now you are totally stoked to tap into your inner Valley Girl. You will need five rad essential pieces to bring your look together head to toe.

All of your Valley Girl fashion pieces need to be pink, aqua, and striped.

First, find a headband to wrap around your forehead.

Find a pair of hoop earrings, the bigger the better.

Your shirt should be loose, neon, and patterned or plain. Bonus for choosing a shirt with a palm tree or California motif.

The only thing small about a Valley Girl's '80s style was her skirt. Choose a miniskirt in neon or denim.

The raddest Valley Girls wore leg warmers over heels with their miniskirts.

I Want My MTV

Pop stars of the radio were brought to TV in 1980. Music Television (MTV) showcased music videos around the clock. It reintroduced some favorites from past generations, such as Michael Jackson. It also introduced new artists such as Madonna, who would go on to set various fashion trends across the '80s and '90s.

Madonna seemed to reinvent herself with every new album release. Though she referred to herself as the Material Girl, her style of the streets attire shifted into high fashion in the 1980s. Madonna's iconic look featured lots of bangle bracelets, a messy tie in her hair, and leggings under a lace skirt.

Perhaps her best addition to fashion was the fingerless lace glove. These gloves differed from those associated with the poor and the tough. Because Madonna's fingerless gloves were made of lace, they were uniquely feminine. Girls of the '80s made their own as they watched Madonna's videos race across their TV screens.

Get the Look

Making fingerless gloves for the very first time? Here's how to copy Madonna's signature early '80s look.

SUPPLIES

- 2 pieces of lace each about twice the size of your palm
- scissors
- sewing supplies

1. Fold each piece of lace in half.
2. Place your hand on top of each folded piece.
3. Measure the pieces so that the folded edge of each piece sits at your knuckles. The bottom of each piece of lace ends at your palm. Cut off any excess material from the bottom edges.
4. Sew the side up. Then sew a hem, or border, around the bottom, leaving the glove open.
5. Cut a hole on the folded side for your thumb after laying your hand on top of the lace to mark where the thumb goes. You may leave the top of the glove open, or you may prefer to sew a small tuck, or closure, between each finger.

Michael Jackson became a star in the 1960s with his brothers in the Jackson 5. Now a young man, Jackson set out on his own. His 1983 album *Thriller* made him an icon in both music and fashion. One of Jackson's signature looks, the single white sparkly glove, debuted in 1983. He wore it during a TV performance of "Billie Jean." His other contribution to fashion was a red zippered jacket created by French designer Claude Montana. It appeared in the music video for the hit song "Beat It." The jacket became so popular there was a high demand for replicas. Red leather jackets have recently been seen on Alicia Keys, Ciara, and Fergie.

Pop sensation Cyndi Lauper also left her mark on '80s style. Neon and dramatic looks highlighted her style. Lauper wore vintage clothing in nontraditional ways. Always bright, her hair color frequently changed shades and was sometimes multicolored, partially shaved, and asymmetric.

Lauper wore her makeup dark and heavy. It featured dramatic splashes of eye shadow and lipstick in red or blue. Her accessories were piled on, with bracelets reaching up and down her arms and many strands of necklaces thrown together. Today's Selena Gomez, Kristen Stewart, and Drew Barrymore love to stack their bracelets.

Get the Look

Cyndi Lauper's mega-hit album, released in 1983, was titled *She's So Unusual.* Anyone sporting Lauper's signature eye makeup is sure to get the same reaction.

SUPPLIES

- bold-colored eye shadows
- eye shadow brush
- black eyeliner
- dark mascara

1. Choose an electric blue color and a secondary color that mismatches the blue, like orange or teal green.
2. Apply the electric blue eye shadow on the entire eyelid, from lashes to brow.
3. Apply that mismatched second color just below the brow line.
4. To further accent your eyes, choose black eyeliner with dark mascara, and "time after time," you'll look like Cyndi Lauper.

Stoked to Get Fit

Alongside the yuppie movement of the 1980s, a trend toward more casual dress was taking place. Like today's yoga wear turned casual fashion, popular sports and the fitness craze made their mark on '80s fashion. Wearing sneakers and workout attire outside the gym became acceptable.

Two major fashion trends to come out of the '80s fitness craze were leg warmers and leotards, especially in bright neon colors. The most popular exercise fad was aerobics, which included high-impact exercises with constant jumping, dancing, and muscle strengthening. Aerobics instructors led their classes while wearing headbands, tights, and legwarmers.

The tights aerobics instructors brought to '80s fashion grew into dressier looks in the form of leggings. And if you've worn a pair of leggings recently, you know these staples of '80s style were not left behind. But leggings of today do have some differences from their '80s ancestors. Leggings of the '80s had even wilder neon patterns. They were also worn with sweaters and oversized blazers.

Stars of today, like Sofia Vergara, right, wear their leggings dressed up with high heels. Others, including Eva Longoria, left, wear theirs more casually with boots for a fashion-forward look on the go.

Perhaps there is no better example of pop culture, fitness, and fashion merging than the 1983 movie *Flashdance.* Jennifer Beals' cutoff collar sweatshirt became the film's signature look. The cutoff collar allowed the sweatshirt to slouch and fall off her shoulders. The look became popular off screen.

Some of the *Flashdance* influence can be seen today. Celebrities such as Victoria Beckham, Katie Holmes, and Lauren Conrad pair skinny jeans with asymmetrical tops. These lop-sided tops hang loosely around the shoulders and taper to a snug fit at the hips.

Get the Look

Make your own *Flashdance* sweatshirt just as Jennifer Beals did.

SUPPLIES

- cotton sweatshirt
- scissors
- ruler
- pencil

1. Shrink the sweatshirt in the dryer so that its collar barely fits over your head. This will make the sweatshirt fit more flatteringly across your body.
2. Lay it flat for measuring and cutting.
3. Measure and mark with a pencil 1 inch (2.5 cm) above the cuffs of the sweatshirt.
4. Measure and mark two to three inches away from the collar of the sweatshirt. This will make the sweatshirt slouch to one side.
5. Cut the lines above the cuffs, and cut the collar out.

'80s Hairstyles

No discussion of '80s fashion is complete without mentioning a few more very large hairstyles. Many women found adding curl essential to their 'do. Perms, which meant treating hair with chemicals to produce curls, were a popular part of large hairdos. Teenagers, moms, guys in '80s hairbands, and professional men and women wore perms to give their hair lots of volume. The tighter the spiral, and the messier you could comb it out, the better. Jennifer Hudson recently sported a less messy perm.

Many men sported a signature '80s hairstyle called the mullet. Mullets were cut short at the front but kept long in the back. A popular phrase called it "business in the front, party in the back." The '80s female answer to the male mullet was the equally voluminous "wall of bangs." For women, the wall of bangs were teased and sprayed to perfection, often curled down, up, and sideways. Though current styles have yet to reach '80s heights, there has been a recent trend to cut bangs into long and short hairstyles. First Lady Michelle Obama, Taylor Swift, Kaley Cuoco, and Olivia Wilde sport bangs with longer cuts.

Get the Look

Reach new heights of hair excellence by creating your own wall of bangs. Remember the goal of large '80s bangs curl and spray them as high as they'd go. You'll want to use a lot of hair spray because once these things fall, look out!

SUPPLIES

- 1-inch (2.5 cm) curling iron
- strong-hold hair spray

1. Divide your bangs into two sections horizontally.
2. Take a 1-inch (2.5-cm) curling iron and curl the top half of the bangs straight up. It sometimes helps to add a touch of hair spray before curling to make sure the curl sticks.
3. Curl the bottom half straight under.
4. Take your fingers and separate the top half so that you get as much volume out of that top piece as possible. You can also curl the sides and feather them back with your fingers, making your bangs extend as far up, down, and to the sides as possible.
5. Spray, tease, and spray some more.

IT'S ALL GOOD: THE 1990S

If the key word of the 1980s was *excess,* the 1990s were more about simplicity. Another important word for the '90s was *change*. A new worldview, alternative styles of music, and a more casual sense of style spread throughout the decade.

Many changes took place throughout the world. With the birth of the Internet, communication across international borders was even easier. As the world shrank, fashion more easily moved from country to country.

Where fashion was once limited to certain regions, the opening of many major retailers abroad meant that clothing styles were shared.

In August 1990, Iraqi military forces invaded Kuwait, setting off Operation Desert Shield. A feeling of patriotic pride swept through the United States. People wore red, white, and blue. The American flag became popular on dresses, shirts, and jackets.

Get the Look

One '90s trend in accessories has politics to thank. The thick headband was most famously worn by then First Lady Hillary Rodham Clinton. Although the design has changed, the stiff headbands of yesterday are back in style today.

SUPPLIES

- 2-inch (5-cm) wide plastic headband
- hot glue gun
- scrap of fabric large enough to cover the headband

1. Line up your fabric, stretching it over the top of the headband with an extra half inch of fabric at both ends of the headband. The glued seam will be under the headband, so smooth out the top before gluing.
2. Start at one end of the headband and apply glue to that side.
3. Quickly press the edge of fabric over the glue and smooth it out down the length of the underside of the headband.
4. Pull the next side tightly so no bumps appear on top of your headband.
5. Apply glue down the second side.
6. Keeping the fabric tight, press it down over the second line of glue.
7. To finish up the ends, fold them inward under the headband and glue both sides.

2013 USA GIRLS GYMNASTICS TEAM

PAULA ABDUL

The hair scrunchie, another accessory favored by everyone from Hillary Clinton to '90s pop star Paula Abdul, has recently reappeared. These accessories are elastic ponytail holders with gathered fabric that is made to stand out as it holds the ponytail in place.

Some of the Team USA girls gymnasts wore scrunchies on the gold medal podium at the London Olympics. During a 2012 fashion show, all the models wore them on the runway. Designer Marc Jacobs has even added colorfully printed scrunchies to his Marc by Marc Jacobs line.

Get the Look

Two things were certain at the beginning of the '90s. First, the United States loved red, white, and blue. Second, if you didn't have a scrunchie with you at all times, that might signal a fashion disaster. To show off your '90s savvy and your patriotism, make your own red, white, and blue scrunchie.

SUPPLIES

- patriotically colored fabric
- sewing materials
- 6-inch (15-cm) piece of elastic

1. Cut your fabric into a piece 4 inches (10 cm) wide and 20 inches (50 cm) long.
2. Fold the fabric in half lengthwise so that the printed side faces inward.
3. Sew only the side seem.
4. Turn the fabric pattern-side out and insert a 6-inch (15-cm) piece of elastic through the fabric tube. The elastic should stretch so that it touches and is sewn to each end of the fabric tube.
5. Put one end of the tube over the other end and stitch them together to make your stylin' '90s scrunchie.

SANDRA BULLOCK

COLOR Blocking

A current clothing trend revived from the 1990s is color blocking. Color blocking means using solid colored clothing to emphasize the best body features. Colors are typically dramatically different. In the '90s it might have been black and white paired together. Models such as Cindy Crawford used the style to highlight their physiques. Now celebrities such as Kim Kardashian and Sandra Bullock have brought the color blocking style back to illustrate their chic sense of style. Today color blocking means pairing colors with their extreme opposites.

PUT IT TOGETHER

You can easily build your own '90s color-blocking outfit. Start with two colors—one that is neutral and one that is bright. A neutral color would be black, gray, white, or beige. Examples of bright colors are green, blue, purple, orange, and pink. Make sure the clothing pieces you choose have no prints.

Many color blocked shirts of the '90s were silk, so choose a silky, flowing blouse or shirt. Pick a color like bright blue for your top.

Pair with a white skirt or neutral colored skirt.

To accessorize, choose a third color that is different from the bright color you chose in the first step. An orange purse and purple shoes will complement the bright blue top and white skirt.

Goodbye Yuppies, Hello Generation X

Fashion of the '80s showed the decade's riches. Fashion of the '90s, however, was affected by a recession and high unemployment. Clothing stores began offering major discounts to attract customers. Designers faced with financial cuts used cheaper fabrics, such as cotton. Young people of the '90s, called Generation X, were highly educated but underemployed. They preferred to buy clothing at bargain prices in thrift stores. Vintage clothing from the 1960s and 1970s, such as cardigan sweaters and worn, faded jeans, became popular. Kristen Stewart and Selena Gomez give worn, comfortable clothing a chic new twist.

PUT IT TOGETHER

To go grunge from top to bottom, start with a beanie hat in a dark color. It's important that you wear your beanie back on the crown of your head rather than pulled down over the forehead.

Wear heavily applied black eyeliner and bright red lipstick. Paint your nails black.

Choose a plaid flannel shirt with the buttons open the whole way down. Put it over a faded T-shirt.

Put on worn out jeans. The more rips and holes in your jeans, the more legitimately grunge you've gone. For that added grunge Gen X-er flair, take the flannel off and tie it loosely around your waist.

Finish your grunge girl look with combat boots or clunky Mary Janes.

Punk + Hippie = Grunge, "Oh well, whatever, nevermind"

In 1991 the band Nirvana released the single "Smells Like Teen Spirit." For teenagers across the United States, this song was their introduction to the grunge movement.

Grunge is a type of music that started in the Pacific Northwest. Beginning in the late '80s, artists such as Nirvana, Pearl Jam, and Soundgarden introduced grunge to mainstream America. The music mixed rock and roll with heavy metal and punk. Its musicians rejected typical '80s values of materialism and excess. Their look came directly from thrift stores and army surplus stores.

Grunge musicians dressed in ripped and faded jeans, long underwear under T-shirts, or old T-shirts under flannels. They also wore Doc Martens or old army boots, beanies over long, straggly hair, and cargo pants.

Typically described as lonely, lost, and bored, followers of the grunge movement rejected the go-getter ideology of the 1980s. Current celebrities such as Rihanna, Gwen Stefani, and Nicole Richie still favor the heavy boots and plaids that embodied the grunge style.

BABES IN TOYLAND 1992

Get the Look

Get easy, no-fuss, grungy hair.

1. Put your hair in a ponytail while it is still wet.
2. As it starts to dry, take the ponytail out. Leave the rubber band marks where they are.
3. Let the flyaways fly free.
4. Don't mess with your hair mess. Leave the brush on the counter so your hair looks as natural and unkempt as possible.

ASHLEY OLSEN

KRISTEN STEWART

ALL THAT AND A BAG OF CHIPS

Fashion designer Calvin Klein had predicted the '90s would be less showy than the '80s. His insight turned out to be quite true. Fashion became more about the look of everyday people. Trends shifted to a more casual look. This comfortable and informal dress contrasted the large shoulder pads and extreme designs of the '80s. Businesspeople began dressing in more casual attire at work. This led to an increase in khaki. The '90s also brought a greater use of denim.

BRITNEY SPEARS 1998

If You Stop by Gap, I'll Come With ...

No retail store is a better example of this shift to casual than Gap. Gap opened in 1969 but grew more popular in the '90s. With its casual clothing and stylish image, the Gap look dominated '90s style.

In the '90s, however, many people preferred khaki to denim. Khaki pants, T-shirts, and neutral colors like grays, tans, whites, and blacks became staples in many closets. These neutral colors contrasted the '80s need for neon. Since the demand for comfortable fashion had increased after the 1980s, signature denim became popular. Bootcut jeans were the most popular cut to come out of the '90s. They featured a flared leg that was less dramatic than the bell-bottoms of the '60s and '70s. These same casual signatures are still popular today. Logo shirts and sweatshirts, denim, and casual khakis are rolled out every season and are seen on celebs such as Kristen Bell, Hilary Swank, and Gwyneth Paltrow.

Babydolls Aren't Just for Toddlers

Simple dresses were also a 1990s fad. The babydoll dress was particularly popular following the grunge movement. Celebrities such as grunge queen Courtney Love made the babydoll dress a popular, somewhat edgy fashion choice. Its empire waistline sits above where the waist naturally falls. The short hem gave it the appearance of a typical toy doll dress. Babydoll dresses could be worn on their own or paired with tights. Many '90s tights had lace around the ankle. Tights with and without lace have come back in style today. The babydoll dress itself remains popular with celebrities such as Carrie Underwood and Jennifer Hudson, and designers such as Stella McCartney.

Another popular dress of the '90s was the simple A-line style. This dress was narrower at the top, gradually falling into a wider bottom, like the letter A. The A-line dress looks flattering on every body type. It has been seen on modern actresses from Octavia Spencer to Sarah Hyland. The '90s made long skirts fashionable. Many of these skirts were covered with floral prints based on vintage patterns. The length of the skirt combined with the detailed pattern created a slimming effect. It hid any body type underneath it.

Underwear Becomes Outerwear

Madonna's look underwent another change at the beginning of the '90s. Her *Blonde Ambition* world tour featured her in designer Jean Paul Gaultier's conical bra and corset. This sparked the '90s "underwear as outerwear" craze. Most fashion followers weren't willing to pair a bra with pants and call it an outfit. But many wore sheer fabric shirts with lace camis, bodysuits, or bustiers underneath.

This "see through" look also inspired spiderweb sweaters, which are wide-woven with some type of tank or cami underneath. Now back in style, they are paired with less risqué lingerie underneath. Selena Gomez regularly wears her UNIF Ashbury crochet dress. Julianne Hough has been seen in a see-through Rag & Bone Exeter crewneck sweater made of lamb's wool.

Hip-Hop Fashion Is Da Bomb

Just as grunge influenced '90s style, hip-hop music entered the American mainstream and brought its fashions with it. There was a new interest in soul, funk, and rap. The look of its artists spread across cultures. Everywhere people began wearing baggy pants and extra-large shirts. Rapper MC Hammer popularized parachute pants. They were often paired with heavy black shoes. Both men and women loved bib overalls. The popular trend at the time had followers wearing either one or both straps down. Wearers included members of the R&B group TLC and hip-hop group Salt-n-Pepa.

Though hip-hop styles have changed, today's hip-hop fashion icons such as Nicki Manaj and M.I.A. still value statement jewelry and other accessories.

PUT IT TOGETHER

Here is your head-to-toe guide to '90s hip-hop style as spun by Salt-n-Pepa.

large door-knocker earrings, preferably gold colored, and choose even larger thick rope gold chain necklaces stacked over top of each other

color blocked silk bomber jackets

acid wash jeans

black or colored boots

AS IF! Pop Culture Trends that Built '90s Fashion

> Fashion of the '90s was heavily influenced by TV and film.

Fashion of the '90s was heavily influenced by TV and film. No film better portrayed the decade's fashions than 1995's *Clueless*. Alicia Silverstone plays a Beverly Hills student with an endless closet.

Clueless contributed many styles to '90s fashion, such as knee-high socks with platform Mary Jane shoes and plaid miniskirts. Perhaps *Clueless*'s most famous fashion contributions, however, were simple, short dresses. They had no pattern or decoration, thin straps, and were very tight.

The dress was well-tailored without lots of extra puffs and fabric. In November 2012 Rihanna wore a red reproduction of this dress to the GQ Men of the Year party.

Of many TV shows that influenced the decade's fashion, one was the sitcom *Blossom.* It brought a playful, vintage-inspired style to a preteen audience. Blossom's signature look was a hat with a large, fake flower on the front. This hat became quite popular, coining the term "Blossom hat."

Get the Look

To make your own Blossom hat, you will need just three supplies and to follow three easy steps.

SUPPLIES

- a small velvet or colored straw hat
- a hot glue gun and glue sticks
- a large craft flower

1. Make sure the brim of your hat is folded back. If it is not, simply roll it up. You may need to reinforce this now bent brim with some hot glue.
2. Take the craft flower and glue it to the front at the center of the hat. The flower should be a vibrant color so that it stands out from the hat.
3. When the glue has set, wear your Blossom hat straight down on your head with bangs and hair peeking straight out.

MAYIM BIALIK
BLOSSOM

Cropped Tops and the Rachel

Beverly Hills, 90210 set several fashion trends. Babydoll dresses and cobweb sweaters were popular at the fictional West Beverly High. *90210* also popularized the half shirt, which was a cropped T-shirt showing the midriff. Celebrities such as Rhianna and Kendall Jenner have recently been spotted in half shirts.

Friends featured the three female characters who sported different looks that reflected their personalities. One already fashionable trend that was popularized by the show was the cropped sweater. It could either be short or long-sleeved and hit above the navel. Popular character Rachel Green often wore her cropped tops with cargo pants as singer Gwen Stefani does today. Some of the signature *Friends* looks included long skirts, bib overalls, and transparent shirts with strappy tops or camis underneath. *Friends* also popularized mock turtlenecks, sweaters and sweater vests, and knee-high boots with miniskirts. No greater trend came out of *Friends* than the infamous haircut dubbed "the Rachel." The mid-length choppy layered hairstyle was copied worldwide after Jennifer Aniston's character Rachel Green began wearing it in 1995. Fans the world over insisted on getting "the Rachel." People still take cues from celebrity hairstyles, whether it is Kerry Washington's faux bob or Michelle Williams' short pixie cut.

JENNIFER ANISTON

PRINCESS DIANA

New Statements of the '90s

By the mid-1990s the marriage of Prince Charles and Princess Diana was over. The royal divorce of 1996 ended Princess Diana's fairy tale, but it freed her style. She no longer needed to follow royal rules about what was appropriate. Her necklines became lower and her skirts shorter. She began wearing sleeveless shift dresses, which were simple dresses that hung straight from the shoulders with no defined waist.

Perhaps the most famous dress Diana wore in the '90s was a form-fitted black dress with a plunging neckline. Diana's daring new look reflected the global shift in women's fashion that was taking place. Women of the '90s were becoming more confident. As a result, they demanded that their clothing showcased their healthy female forms. Today celebrities such as Angelina Jolie aren't afraid to show a little, or a lot of leg, as she did in her black Versace at the 2012 Academy Awards.

ANGELINA JOLIE

6

RETRO FASHIONS ARE MODERN FASHIONS

From the roaring '20s to the preppy '90s, fashion has evolved through the decades. Hemlines lifted from calves to thighs. Form-fitting clothing celebrated the female body. Styles change but one thing remains the same—the trends of the past continue to influence the fashions of the future.

Miniskirts, leggings, and power suits are just a few of the fashions we can thank the past decades for. Women still wear suits to work and little black dresses for special occasions.

Bias cuts and A-lines still flatter different body types. Scarves and beaded necklaces remain popular accessories on and off the red carpet.

From pop stars to politicians, fashion influences come from everywhere. And they can come from you too. Don't be afraid to be daring with your own personal style. Be creative when putting together your own looks. Try changing up old trends to create something new. Maybe you will become the next fashion forward designer.

RETRO
FASHIONS

Index

Adrian, Gilbert, 62
Balenciaga, Cristóbal, 84
bombshell look, 96, 98, 100
Cassini, Oleg, 108
Chanel, Coco, 5, 18, 19, 20, 24, 28, 64, 82
Dali, Salvador, 46, 47, 48, 50, 52
Dior, Christian, 80, 82, 86
dresses
- A-line, 108, 196, 206
- babydoll, 196, 202
- little black dress (LBD), 24, 64, 206
- minidresses, 114, 115, 122, 124, 143
- popover, 64, 74
- sack, 84, 108
- sheath, 64, 65
- shift, 108, 204

Emmanuel, David and Elizabeth, 156
Factor, Max, 100
Ferragamo, Salvatore, 71, 72
glam look, 138, 139, 140, 141, 142, 160
greaser look, 86, 88, 103
Great Gatsby look, 20, 21, 26, 27
grunge look, 191, 192, 193, 196, 198
hairstyles
- afro, 126
- beehive, 127
- bobs, 12, 28, 38, 202
- chignons, 60, 61
- Farrah flip, 151
- finger waves, 38–39
- mullets, 182
- peek-a-boo, 102
- perms, 182
- pompadour, 103
- the Rachel, 202
- spit curls, 60
- wall of bangs, 182, 183

hood look, 88, 89
Klein, Calvin, 150, 194
Lauren, Ralph, 34, 149
makeup, 4, 12, 14, 43, 96, 100, 101, 117, 140, 141, 144, 160, 166, 177, 176
masculine look, 44, 45
McCardell, Claire, 64, 92–93
Montana, Claude, 176
Norell, Norman, 64, 65
pants
- bell-bottoms, 134, 195
- cargo, 192, 202
- khaki, 33, 149, 195
- jeans, 4, 88, 89, 128, 132, 133, 134, 135, 139, 150, 154, 180, 190, 191, 192, 195, 199
- parachute, 198
- sailor, 34

Patou, Jean, 20, 22
preppy look, 172, 206
Pucci, Emilio, 119
punk look, 4, 144, 145, 160, 161, 162
Quant, Mary, 112, 114
Rabanne, Paco, 122
Saint Laurent, Yves, 148
Schiaparelli, Elsa, 46, 48, 49, 50, 52
shoes
- boots, 144, 145, 154, 161, 179, 191, 192, 199, 202
- Mary Janes, 17, 30, 57, 114, 191, 200
- saddle, 87, 90, 95
- sandals, 72–73, 128, 131, 142
- sneakers, 88, 178

skirts
- maxi, 128, 147
- miniskirt, 112, 114, 128, 147, 154, 173, 200, 202, 206
- pencil, 17, 66, 82
- poodle, 90–91

sportswear, 18, 20, 21, 22, 92, 94–95, 172, 178
surreal styles, 46, 48, 50, 52–53
Ungaro, Emmanuel, 122
Vanderbilt, Gloria, 150
Vionnet, Madeleine, 42
Von Furstenberg, Diane, 150
Westwood Vivienne, 160

Photo Credits

123RF: Oleksii Sergieiev, 131; Alamy Images: AF archive, 98, Everett Collection, Inc., 20 (r), 82 (l), Martyn Goddard, 144 (l), Moviestore Collection, 200 (l), Pictorial Press Ltd., 140, Redsnapper, 172, Trinity Mirror/Mirrorpix, 164, 178; AP Images: Rex Features, 143 (b); Artresource, N.Y.: The Metropolitan Museum of Art, 48 (b), 64, 84 (l); Bridgeman Artlibrary: Christie's Images, 122, Philadelphia Museum of Art, 50; Capstone Studio: Karon Dubke, 9 (b), 11, 13, 17, 21, 27, 29, 36, 37, 41, 47, 49, 51, 61, 65, 69, 72, 73, 75, 79, 85, 87, 91, 109, 111, 113, 120, 121, 123, 125, 127, 129, 133, 135, 137, 165, 167, 181, 185, 187; Corbis: Bettmann, 8 (l), 92, 119 (t), 134 (l), 146, CinemaPhoto, 180 (r), Conde Nast Archive, 24, David Lees, 71, Hermlewis/Kipa, 203, Lynn Goldsmith, 136 (l), Mauro Carraro/Sygma, 190 (l), Splash News, 95 (t), Vittoriano Rastelli, 168 (l); Dreamstime: Phildate, 171; Getty Images: ABC Photo Archives, 166 (b), Alfred Eisenstaedt/Time & Life Pictures, 62, 70-71, Alinari Archives, Florence, 18, Anwar Hussein, 157, Artrickerby/Time Life Pictures, 107 (l), Bert Hardy/Picture Post/Hulton Archive, 66 (l), Bill Ray/Time Life Pictures, 148, Brian Smith/Bride Lane Library/Popperfoto, 162 (r), Bruce Gilkas/FilmMagic, 152 (r), Central Press, 44 (l), Chicago History Museum, 7, China Pix, 180 (l), ChinaFotress, 188, Dean Conger/The Denver Post, 78 (l), Dirck Halsteat/Time & Life Pictures, 162 (l), Donato Sardellia/WireImage, 28 (m), Ebertroberts/Redferns, 160 (l), Emmanuel Dun&/AFP, 186 (t), Evelyn Floret/Time Life Pictures, 150, Evening St&ard, 130, Fin Costello/Redferns, 142, FPG/Hulton Archive, 14, George Hurrell/John Kobal Foundation, 97, George Marks/Retrofile, 77, General Photographic Agency, 31 (tl), Harold M. Lambert, 74, Harry Langdon, 201, Henry Groskinsky/Time Life Pictures, 151, Hulton Archive, 12 (t), 25 (b), 112, 118, 126 (r), 152 (l), 170, Imagno, 23, 42 (l), James Devaney/WireImage, 28 (r), 35, Janette Beckman, 198, Jayne Fincher, 204, Jean Baptiste Lacroix/WireImage, 160 (r), Jean-Claude Deutsch/Paris Match, 132 (l), Jef Kravitz/FilmMagic, 53 (l), Jeffrey Ufbert/WireImage, 119 (b), Jesse Grant/WireImage, 19 (l), Jim Smeal/WireImage, 197 (r), John D. Kisch/Separate Cinema Archive, 138, John Keystone-France/Gamma-Keystone, 80, Kathleen Revis/National Geographic, 86, Kevin Cummins/Premium Archive, 192, Kevin Mazur Archive/WireImage, 194, 196 (l), Keystone, 110 (l), Kobal Foundation, 5 (bl), 40 (l), 102 (l), Mark Rucker/Transcendental Graphics, 94, Mia Junior/BuzzFoto, 197 (l), Michel Dufour/WireImage, 82 (r), Michael Ochs Archives, 143 (t), 182 (l), Michael Putl&, 174, Popperfoto/Bob Thomas, 20 (l), 116, RDA, 108 (r), Rolls Press/Popperfoto, 5 b m), 124, 128, Ron Galella Collection, 25 (tl), 183, 186 (b), Sasha, 26 (r), 30, Steve Granitz/WireImage, 93 (l), Terry Lott/Sony Music Archive, 176 (t), Tim Graham, 25 (tm), 158 (t), Time Life Pictures/Mansell, 32 (l), Vernon Merritt III/Time Life Pictures, 114, Warner Brothers, 88 (l); House of Francheska, 46; iStockphoto: ARSELA, 189, eliferen, 33, ilzesgimene, 57, Yurdakul, 35; Library of Congress, 22 (b); Newscom: Doug Meszier/Splash News, 134 (r), 154 (m), London Entertainment/Splash, 179 (r), smg/Finalpixx, 193 (l), Solo/ZUMA Press, 52 (l); Shutterstock: Adam Glickman/Underwood Archives, 58, Adisa, 65, 139, Africa Studio, 45, 145, Alan Poulson Photography, 33, Aleksei Smolensky, 145, 191, Allan Grant/Time Life Pictures, 100, &ersphoto, 63 (l), angelo gilardelli, 15 (t), Anna Lurye, cover, Anna Tyukhemneva, design, anneka, 16, anyamuse, 199, Apostrophe, design, Artter, 191, Azuzl, design, Brooke Becker 115, Buida Nikita Yourievich, 115, BW Folsom, 145, caimacanul, 45, catwalker, 52 (r), Cherkas, 65, Craig Wactor, 145, cretolamna, 57, DFree, 103, Dinodia, 60 (l), Dostoevsky, 83, Eky Studio, design, El Greco, 21, Eleonora Kolomiyets, design, elic, design, Elnur, 83, 89, 107, 149, 189, EM Arts, 161, Everett Collection, 28 (l), 31 (mr), 34, 95 (b), faithie, 141 (l), Featureflash, 5 (br & tl), 12 (b), 15 (bl), 32 (r), 40 (r), 42 (r), 53 (r), 54 (m & r), 55 (r), 84 (r), 93 (r), 102 (r), 104 (r), 105 (l), 110 (r), 117 (r), 126 (l), 132 (r), 147 (r), 155 (r), 158 (b), 193 (r), 205, FramAngel, cover, 17, Gavran333, 169, Glamour, 89, Gnilenkov Aleksey, 67 (b), Gordana Sermek, 21, 33, grynold, 31 (ml), Gulei Ivan, 153, Hakan Kizitan, 31 (bl), happykanppy, design, Hector Sanchez, 19 (m), Helga Esteb, 8 (r), 25 (tr), 60 (r), 99 (m), 104 (l), Helga Pataki, design, Hugo Felix, 184, Ivaschenko Roman, 131, Jaguar PS, 48 (t), 88 (r), 154 (l), 166 (t), 195 (l), Joe Seer, 15 (br), 39, 55 (l), 104 (m), 168 (r), 190 (r), 196 (r), 200 (r), Juergen Faelchie, design, Karkas, cover, 17, 21, 31 (tm), 57, 65, 83, 89, 107, 115, 149, 169, 189, kavring, 83, kedrov, 115, Kletr, 139, Korionov, 159, L.F., 31 (tr), Kotss, 173, Kaya, 89, Lasha, 199, Leila B., 57, 149, Lena Ivanova, 33, Lisovskaya Natalia, 17, Lucy Liu, 89, ludmilafoto, 161, MargoLLL, 107, maxstockphoto, 31 (m), 173, Michael Kraus, 131, Mitrofanova, 169, Nadja Antonova, 107, NataLT, 175 (r), Natalia Litovchenko, design, Natalia Matveeva, 31 (br), Natykach Natalia, design, Nejron Photo, 38, Nicole Weiss, 141 (tr), Nito, 173, Oksancia, design, Olena Zaskochenko, 9 (t), Olga Ekaterincheva, 43, 117 (l), OZaiachin, 191, pashabo, design, Petr Malyshev, 161, Photobank.ch, 199, PhotoNAN, 139, Photo Works, 15 (b), Picsfive, 145, Pietus, design, pix4u, 115, pil76 175 (l), Poitr Krzeslak, design, ppart, 115, Prapann, 131, Rene Schild, 22 (t), Richard Peterson, 21, 173, Roberto Castillo, design, Roman Samokhin, 199, Ruslan Kudrin, 145, 149, 161, 191, 199, s_bukley, 5 (tr), 44, 54 (l) (r), 59, 63 (r), 66 (r), 67 (t), 78 (r), 81, 99 (l & r), 101, 105 (r), 108 (l), 136 (r), 144 (r), 147 (l), 154 (r), 155 (l), 163, 176 (b), 179 (l), 195 (r), 202, 207 (l & r), sagir, 21, 45, 57 (l), 153, Set, 149, Schab, 169, Serg Zastavkin, 177, Sergey Peterman, 153, Sharon Alex&er, 19 (r), spillman, 45, Spotlight, 182 (r), Stargazer, design, tanuha2001, 67 (m), Teeratas, 107, worldswildlifewonders, 26 (l), Yeko Photo Studio, 141 (br), Zaneta Baranowska, 83